MW01089027

JUST RIGHT

The Road from Addiction to Redemption

By

Barbara Bice

www.xulonpress.com

Dedication

On Sunday, September 27, 2012, my precious mother passed away at the age of ninety-four. She was a Godly woman who lived a long and faithful life until the very end. It seemed so appropriate to me that our heavenly Father called her home on a Sunday, His day. She was a loving mother, a constant inspiration to me, an amazing example of love and patience, and an angel in my life. I dedicate this book to her. Before she went to be with the Lord, she told me she read the manuscript draft not only once, but twice.

CONTENTS

ACKNOWLEDGMENTS

For a long time, I toyed with the thought of one day writing a book. However, it was not until after our good friend, Allen, encouraged me to do so that I began giving it serious thought. Allen heard me tell a brief part of my story at church and afterwards said, "You really need to write a book about all of this. You should write your side of the story, and Ed should write his side of the story." Although I could never get Ed onboard with that idea, it motivated me to start writing. That very night I went home, quickly wrote the first chapter, and then got "writer's block."

I began to pray about the book. I asked God to help me remember things—things I had previously asked Him to help me forget. I also prayed He would give me direction, wisdom, clear thoughts, and words for just one more chapter. Many nights, I fell asleep praying for God to help me with the book, and I would wake up in the middle of the night with words and thoughts fresh on my mind to write.

My sister, Brenda, was my constant cheerleader. She called me regularly to see if I was still "working" on the book. She kept motivating me to write a new chapter; then as soon as she would finish reading that chapter, she would start encouraging me to write one more. She prayed for the book and her motivation truly kept me writing. Without her ongoing encouragement, I might not have ever completed the book.

I thank my brother, Rick, and his wife, Louise, (Weezie to us) for their encouragement, love, prayers, and for reminding me of some things I had forgotten.

I am grateful to Buddy and Al for taking time to read my manuscript and for their sweet words and very kind reviews for my book cover.

I designated my longtime friend, Amy, as my "unofficial" editor. Amy spent many, many hours reading and re-reading my drafts. She proofed and corrected my grammar, my spelling, my margins, and my "fonts." Many times we were on the telephone late at night talking about the book and ways to improve it. Her friendship, help, encouragement, and prayers throughout this process have been immeasurable.

I thank my sweet friend, Norma, for reading and putting her stamp of approval on the "Storms" chapter. Norma and I share a bond. Though the tornado in her life and the tornado in my life were very different, we are both "storm survivors."

My dear friends, Ramona, Faith Ann, and Linda read the first and final drafts. They were my "test run." They brainstormed with me over the book and gave me so many words of encouragement. They, too, prayed for me and prayed for the book. I will always remember the phone calls and emails I received from these special friends after they read the very first draft of the book. Each told me of how the book impacted them. I was totally blown away. Though they may not remember the words they spoke to me, I will never forget.

I am thankful to Katie for her time, help, and expertise in getting the book ready for the publisher.

A very special thank you to Joe for his kindness, patience and expertise in creating my book cover. To me, it is perfect.

Although I had a couple of really good suggestions for the book title, when Linda told me that after praying, *Just Right* came to her, I knew that was it. Many times I grew anxious about finding a way to get the book published, and

Linda would always tell me she was "praying it through." She once told me, "Writing and publishing a book is like birthing a baby. It takes time, patience, and it's painful." She was so right.

The most difficult part of this process was when I emailed the final draft to my sons and their wives. I waited anxiously to hear back from them. I knew the book contained some things they would be learning for the first time. I was extremely nervous that they might not approve of the book. However, one by one, they called me with words of love and encouragement. They inspired me to move forward.

Although Ed and I are characters in this book, the book is really not intended to be about us. It is intended to be a story about how our gracious heavenly Father rescues people, changes hearts and restores lives.

I have no idea how many people will ever read this book, but I believe with all my heart that God wants me to tell this story. So, whether this book reaches one person or one thousand people, if you are reading it, I do not believe it is by accident.

CHAPTER 1

The Road

$\mathcal{I}$ rolled over in bed and laid my head on his pillow. Although I was exhausted, sleep would not come. I looked at the clock for the hundredth time that night. Midnight. One o'clock. One-twenty. Two-fifteen. I prayed, I cried, and I prayed some more. "Please God, don't let him be doing it again."

I got out of bed and walked over to the bedroom doors that led to a large deck. "This was supposed to be our dream home," I thought to myself. It sat almost in the middle of fifteen acres. As I looked out into the night, the moon was so full and so bright. I felt I could see every tree, every rise and slope of the land . . . and every shadow. I thanked God for the bright moon because I knew I would be going out into the night alone again. I reluctantly got dressed and went upstairs where our sons were sleeping.

I hated myself for what I was about to do, but what other choice did I have? I did not want to wake my son, but suppose one of the boys woke up and needed me? Suppose the house caught on fire after I left? I had to tell someone I was leaving. I knelt down beside his bed, said a silent prayer, and then, for what seemed like the millionth time, I gently shook our middle son and whispered to him, "I'll be back soon." My heart broke because I knew he knew what that meant. For so long I tried to hide the truth from our sons to protect them, to cover it up, but by this time, he knew something was wrong. All three sons knew something was terribly wrong. Yet, I still wanted so badly to spare them the heartache I was feeling . . . that gut-wrenching raw fear I felt every time he did not come home.

I got into my car and headed down the long winding driveway and onto the narrow dirt road that led to the main paved road. As I turned onto the dirt road, I wondered to myself, "Will I find him this time? Where will he be this time? What lies will he tell me this time?" Then, almost instantly, I was overcome with anger at myself that I would even stoop so low as to go looking for him again. Hadn't I had enough already? Then, as I rounded a small curve in the road, I saw headlights. I knew the lights were his. I stopped my car and waited. As he drove closer, I turned off the engine and headlights, got out of the car, and stood in the middle of the dusty dirt road.

I watched as he brought his truck to a stop some distance in front of my car. Finally, his headlights went off and he stepped out of the truck. The moon lit up the dirt road like a runway. We walked towards each other slowly. It was like a showdown in a western movie, only I had no weapon to pull. I was again thankful that the moon was so bright because I wanted him to see the disappointment, the anger and most of all the hurt on my face. When I looked into his eyes, I knew beyond a shadow of a doubt he had done it again.

Every promise he made to me died in an instant. "Lies, all lies," I thought. Staring him in the eyes and feeling a rage like I had never felt before, I said to him, "If you ever do it again, I hope it kills you." Tears began to fill his eyes and as I turned to walk away, I heard him say the words that shook me to my very core, "I hope it does, too." he said.

As I finish writing this chapter, I am amazed it has been over twenty years since that night of reckoning. That dusty dirt road was my "road to Damascus." It was where the pieces seemed to fit into place. Like the blind man, my eyes had been opened. "I once was blind, but now I see."

It was that night on that dirt road I realized my husband's addiction to cocaine was much greater and much stronger than either of us could have ever imagined. It was that night I no longer believed what I had often said to him, "If you love me and love your children, you will stop using drugs." I finally realized it was not about love. It was about a life that had spun out of control due to a powerful and ravaging addiction.

It was on that dirt road, on that moonlit night, I realized that without a miracle, my husband was not going to beat this horrible addiction that had consumed his life. Without a miracle, my shroud of despair and hopelessness would never be lifted. Without a miracle, our marriage would never survive all the damage caused by my husband's addiction. Thank God for miracles.

"A second time they summoned the man who had been blind, 'Give glory to God,' they said. 'We know the man is a sinner.' He replied, 'Whether he is a sinner or not, I do not know. One thing I do know. I was blind, but now I see!'" (John 9: 24-26).

"I will lead the blind by ways they have not known, along unfamiliar paths I will guide them; I will turn the darkness into light before them and make the rough places smooth. These are the things I will do; I will not forsake them" (Isaiah 42:16).

CHAPTER 2

Child of an Alcoholic

I am the daughter of an alcoholic. Although my father was sober most of my adult years, I vividly remember many times as a child waking up in the middle of the night to the sound of my father yelling at my mother. Even though I was very young at the time, I remember being in that state of sleep right before I was fully awake and not knowing if it was a bad dream or if it was really happening. I would be praying with every little bone in my body that it was just a bad dream. Then, as the sounds became louder and more intense, I knew it was not a dream.

My parents would always be sitting at the kitchen table. My father would be sitting at one end of the table, and my mother would be sitting at the other end. I remember that kitchen table well. It was the kind of table popular in the fifties. It was similar to what you would see in a diner or café at that time, except it could seat six people. It had a green, somewhat scratched and dented, metal top and six chrome metal chairs with green cushioned seats covered in plastic. Often, my father would bang his fists on the kitchen tabletop as he was yelling at my mother . . . thus, the dents.

Many times I would wake up crying because of the yelling, and I would crawl out of bed and make my way into the kitchen. To this day, I remember the look of fear on my mother's face every time she saw me come into the kitchen where they were. When my father would see me, he would usually start to cry and he would motion for me to come to him. Although my mother's eyes would seem to be saying "No, don't go," I would always go to him, and he would pull me up on his lap. For some reason, I had a temporary calming effect on him.

During these "yelling sessions" between my mother and father, one thing was lacking. My mother never said one word back to him. She would just sit there, often with tears running down her face, but always silent.

My mother was a waitress. She worked the early shift at a downtown café next to the barbershop. As a little girl, I would often get my bangs cut in the barbershop by Snead, the barber. Even now, I am still not sure if Snead was his first or last name. In fact, everyone called him "Snead the Barber" as though that was his full name. He would put a board across the barber chair for me to sit on so I would be tall enough. Every time he finished cutting my bangs, he would give me a dollar. What a deal. . . getting paid to get my hair cut.

My mother would leave our home for work around four o'clock in the morning so that she could get to the café in time to prep for the five-thirty opening. That meant she woke up each workday by three o'clock. I cannot even begin to imagine how hard her job and work hours must have been on her. That, coupled with raising three children and living with an alcoholic husband, must have been overwhelming. Every time I think my life is hectic, I think of her life, and my whining stops.

The only telephone in the café was a pay phone. Back then a call home would cost Mama a whole dime. So if she needed to call home to check on us kids during the day, she would call, let it ring twice, and then hang up. No one at our house ever dared to pick up the telephone before the third ring for fear that Mama would lose her dime. If the rings stopped at two, we always knew it was Mama, and we would call her back. After all, a dime was a dime.

Mama got off work around two-thirty in the afternoon, and by the time she made it home she was exhausted from being on her feet all day. Often she would fall asleep on the couch before having to get back up to cook supper for everyone. After supper each night, she would always iron her starched white uniform and polish her white work shoes until both were perfect. She took a lot of pride in how she looked. I remember one time a little neighborhood boy teased me about my mother being a waitress. I'm not sure why, but perhaps because of the teasing and because I was so young, the next time a friend asked me where Mama worked, I said, "She's a nurse." I guess I thought the white uniform would fool them. One thing was certain; she was a wonderful mother, an extremely hard worker, and a very devoted wife to my father—none of which were easy.

My parents first met at the café where my mother worked. It was across the street from the Police Department. My father was a tall, dark haired, brown-eyed, handsome detective who would often go to the café on his break for lunch or sometimes coffee, but more than likely he went just to see the very pretty dark-haired waitress. My mother and father fell in love and married shortly after they met. She was twenty-nine, and he was thirty. When I was born, my mother was thirty-five. I am the youngest of three children.

My mother was one of nine children, and we would often go to visit her family in Mississippi. My father's mother, father, and siblings were all deceased by the time I was born. However, I know that my father's father had also worked as a policeman; and, like my father, he too was an alcoholic. I learned later in life that when my father was young, his sister died from cancer, his mother died from cancer, and his father's drinking grew worse and worse.

When my father was only sixteen years old, he came home one afternoon from school to discover that his father had simply left and abandoned him. At sixteen, my dad was left to fend for himself. Perhaps he drank because he was the son of an alcoholic and was somehow predisposed to drink. Or maybe it was because of the rejection, abandonment, and heartache he endured. Or maybe it was a combination of it all.

I guess you would say my father was a "functioning" alcoholic. He always managed to hold down a job; and, with the help of my mother's wages and tip money they were able to support the family. When my father was sober, he was a kind, tenderhearted man who would give you the shirt off of his back. He loved to sing old gospel songs, especially when we were going somewhere in the car. I have many memories of my father and sister harmonizing to "Farther Along" and "If I Could Hear My Mother Pray Again" as we rode.

There were times when my father would go for long periods of time without drinking. But when he did drink, he could not and did not stop drinking and was no longer a kind man. There were many times when my mother would have to take him to the hospital because he was "sick." When I became an adult, I learned those times were to detox him.

I remember during one of his binges, he was fussing about the house not being clean enough. I'm sure with my mother working all the time and with three kids at home, the house probably wasn't always clean. However, as a child, I began to think if I kept my room perfectly straight, my father would not drink; and when he did drink, I was sure it was because I did not keep my room clean enough. You see, even though I was very young, I had started to develop those co-dependent traits most family members of alcoholics and addicts develop. I thought that somehow I was doing something to cause him to drink and could therefore do something within my own power to keep him from drinking. Even to this day, I sometimes feel that if my house is in order, my life is in order. Sick thinking? Oh yes. You see, co-dependency may not be a disease in and of itself, but I believe it can make you very sick.

I thank God my father found the rooms of Alcoholics Anonymous. I am not sure how often he attended, but I know for sure that every Tuesday night my mother and father went to an open AA meeting. I remember that so vividly because my brother, sister, and I always looked so forward to Tuesday nights. As soon as our parents left for the AA meeting, we would sneak out of the house and tell ghost stories with some other kids in the neighborhood. We stayed very close to our house so when we saw their car lights coming down the street, we could jump up, run like mad, and make it back inside the house before they could see us. Of course, after I was grown, I learned they had always seen us.

On one of their AA nights, my sister, who was the oldest, but still too young to drive, decided (after much begging and pleading from my brother and me) that she would get our dad's car keys and drive us in his 1953 white Chevrolet to the donut shop for donuts. Back then, it seemed like that car was about the size of a small house. My brother sat up front with my sister, and I sat in the "back wing." Everything went perfectly — just as planned — until we got home and she broke the key off in the ignition. No matter how hard we tried, we never could get away with anything.

My father managed to stay sober for many, many years. Unfortunately, he quit going to his AA meetings and quit doing the things that kept him sober. As a result, he relapsed when I was about sixteen.

My father loved to play golf. In fact, he passed the love of that game on to my sister, brother, and me. The day my dad relapsed was a southern summer day, and it was very hot and humid. He and a few of his golf buddies were on the back nine of the golf course, far from the clubhouse, far from water to drink, and he was very hot and thirsty. A new man in their group, who did not know my father very well, had a cooler with some beer, and he offered my father one. Daddy turned it down at first, but then in one weak moment made the decision that since he had been sober for so long, "just one beer" would not hurt.

The old saying, "One is too many and a hundred is never enough" is so true. Alcoholism is a progressive disease. Even though an alcoholic may go years without drinking, if he or she drinks, the disease picks up as though the alcoholic had never stopped drinking. My dad did not make it home until very late that night, and it was "déjà vu all over again." Different night, different kitchen table, but the same fear.

It took my dad a while to get back into recovery, but I am thankful that when he died in 1982, he died not only a sober man, but a Godly man. Even though he struggled many years with his addiction, he never, ever, gave up. He kept getting back up and trying to do the next right thing. During the time he was sober, he often brought people home to live with us. We once had a recovering drug addict live with us. Another time, we had a recovering alcoholic live with us. Then sometimes, he would just bring young people home straight out of jail if they had nowhere else to go. My dad would mentor them, encourage them, and give them a place to stay until they could get back on their feet. As I reflect back on that today, I see he was working the twelfth step of AA back then: "Having had a spiritual awakening," he was "carrying the message" to others.

I thank God my father stayed strong and did not give up. Yet, as strong as my father was, in my heart the strongest one was my mother. She never wavered in her love for my father, her commitment to him, or her faith in a God whom she knew could change him.

Some of my earliest and fondest memories of my mother are her kneeling at the side of her bed every night and praying. As a child, I would always get very close to her as she prayed. I would put my ear as close as I could to her mouth and try my best to hear what she was saying to God, but I never could make out the words. Today, being married to an addict myself, I'm pretty sure I know exactly what she was praying.

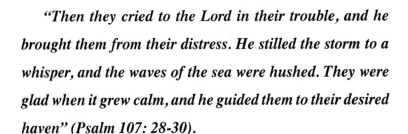

"Then they cried to the Lord in their trouble, and he brought them from their distress. He stilled the storm to a whisper, and the waves of the sea were hushed. They were glad when it grew calm, and he guided them to their desired haven" (Psalm 107: 28-30).

CHAPTER 3

In the Beginning

I saw Ed for the first time when I was twelve years old. Our families attended the same very conservative church, so I saw Ed every Sunday morning, Sunday night, and Wednesday night. When I was fourteen years old, I began to notice Ed more and more. He was tall, thin, good-looking, confident, and always dressed very preppy. But, most importantly, he had a car.

We were, of course, too young to date; but because our families knew each other, it was common for me to go home with him after church on Sundays to have lunch or for him to come to my home for lunch. Even when we did start dating, we had no money, so we usually just "hung out" together at the local hamburger joint, and every now and then we went to a movie.

Ed was twenty and I was seventeen when we got married. As I write that, I cringe to think how young we were. At the time, we thought we were soooooo in love. Looking back (way back), I am sure we loved each other as much as a twenty-year-old and a seventeen-year-old knew how to love.

I will never forget the day my father walked me down the aisle to marry Ed. The closer we got to Ed, the slower my dad walked. When we were about fifteen feet from Ed and the preacher, I thought for sure Daddy was going to come to a complete halt. We were barely moving. In fact, I clearly remember whispering to him out of the side of my mouth, while trying to maintain a smile, "Come on Daddy, please don't stop." My parents approved of me marrying Ed, but I was only seventeen years old, the baby of the family, and it wasn't easy for Daddy to "give me away."

Ed and I lived a very normal life with the usual ups and downs of marriage and raising children. When our three sons were growing up, our days and nights were filled with school, homework, T-ball games, baseball games, and football games. As the years passed, we lived in several different homes, and with each move we improved a little over the last one. One of our favorite homes was on a cul-de-sac where lots of other children lived. Our boys absolutely loved that neighborhood. It was the kind of neighborhood where all the kids played outside, even after dark, without ever worrying about traffic or strangers. All the neighbors knew one another and all of us looked out for each other's children. The most wonderful thing about that neighborhood was that we lived next door to my sister and her family. A lot of evenings, my sister and I would sit in lawn chairs outside while the children played, and we would catch up on the latest gossip, uh, I mean "news."

Ed found and purchased approximately fifteen acres. It had always been his dream to one day buy some land and build a house in the country. While we continued to live on the cul-de-sac, Ed began clearing off part of the land to build our dream home. Many weekends we would take picnic lunches and all go to the property. I would often sit and read a book, or sometimes, just walk around learning the land. The boys would ride four-wheelers while Ed road his tractor and cleared the home site. Oftentimes, he would have the boys help him. With chainsaw in hand, he would say, "Boys, we're going to cut down a few trees today." Ed loved to work in the woods and clear the land. In fact, he loved it so much that I worried he would clear too much. My oldest son recently joked that he was almost grown before he realized that a "few trees" was not the same as a "few acres."

Life in the country was wonderful for the boys. They adapted quickly. It was a haven for them. They hunted squirrels, fished and just explored the woods. There was a creek near our house, and the boys would walk the creek and bring home Indian artifacts such as arrowheads and broken pieces of pottery.

It seemed as if life could not get any better. Then late one night, we received a call that Ed's brother had been seriously injured. When we arrived at the hospital, there was little hope that his brother would live. He had been shot. The bullet had entered his brain and was inoperable. By the grace of God, his brother, after many weeks in the hospital, was able to return home; however, he remained partially paralyzed on one side.

Prior to that incident, Ed's brother owned a successful roofing business, and Ed was a successful salesman for a very large automotive company. For many months, Ed worked his own job as well as working to keep his brother's business running. Although it took a very heavy physical and emotional toll on him, he worked both jobs until it became an impossible load for him to carry. Eventually, Ed made the decision to purchase his brother's business, and Ed resigned from his sales position.

Ed's roofing company became more and more profitable. However, after several years in the roofing business, the profits began to disappear. Although I didn't know it at the time, this was the beginning of Ed's addiction. It was also the beginning of much heartache, much fear, and much loss.

This book is about overcoming that addiction, heartache, fear and loss. I will be the first to admit that I am not a writer by any stretch of the imagination. This is a short, simple book with no flowery or fancy words, but I am writing from my heart. It is not intended to be a "tell all" book. Although it contains some of "the good, the bad, and the ugly," it is my prayer that the overriding message is a message of hope.

"May the God of hope fill you with all joy and peace as you trust in Him, so that you may overflow with hope by the power of the Holy Spirit" (Romans 15:13).

CHAPTER 4

When the Abnormal Becomes Normal

I was standing in line at a department store today when a song by Cheryl Crow came on over the intercom. It's a song many of you may know. It started out, "The first cut is the deepest . . . ." As I listened to the song, those words resonated with me, and I thought to myself, "How very true." The first pain of anything can cut the deepest and hurt the most—your first broken heart, the first time you're not picked for the team, the first time you are passed up for a promotion.

The same is true when you love and/or live with an addict. The first time a husband or wife lies to you; the first time a child staggers in drunk or steals from you; the first time a bill doesn't get paid or the utilities get turned off because the family funds have been used to feed a habit—all of these things initially shock and hurt. Unfortunately, and strangely, the more it happens, the more adept you tend to become even though you hate what is happening. I tell you this because I wish someone had told me this. When my life was spinning out of control and I could not figure out why, I wish someone had said, "Wake up! Your husband is using drugs. Can't you see that?" The truth is that no, I could not see it, because I never expected it to happen. And I never, ever, dreamed such a thing could happen to us.

At first, I was not aware of the signs of addiction; and later, when all the signs of addiction were there, the abnormal had already become normal. This won't make any sense to you unless someone very close to you is an addict or alcoholic. If they are, I can almost hear you say, "She's right." It's like the frog that gets slow-cooked. If you drop the frog into boiling water, it will immediately hop out of the hot water; however, they say if you put him in a pot of cool water and gradually increase the heat, you can cook the frog alive. Have you ever been cooked alive? Metaphorically speaking, of course. I have.

At first the changes in Ed were very subtle. He seemed to be somewhat withdrawn, a bit troubled and sometimes depressed. There was a period after my father's death when I suffered from a bout of depression, so when I started noticing certain changes in Ed, I began to think his brother's poor health and the stress of his new business were catching up with him. Other symptoms often associated with depression began to appear. Ed began to eat and sleep less. Then there were times when all he could do was sleep. There would be times when I would go to work in the morning and come home in the evening, and Ed would still be in the bed. Little did I know, the worst was yet to come.

Too many nights to even remember at this point, Ed was extremely late coming home. His excuse would always be his roofing business. Either he would say he was running late getting back from out of town, or his excuse would be that they were having problems with his roofing equipment. There came a time when I thought Ed had to be either cursed or the most unlucky man in the world because he had so many problems with his dump trucks, tractors, roofing tools, equipment and employees. I felt so sorry for him. Of course, later I would learn that it was never the trucks, tractors, equipment or employees that he was having trouble with. It was drugs.

Often I would wake up in the middle of the night to find that Ed had left. I would call his cell phone, and he would not answer. Usually the next morning I would finally be able to get up with him, and he would always have some unbelievable excuse. But I was so gullible and always believed him. At that point, I still wanted to trust Ed. I just kept telling myself it was the "depression" causing Ed to act so differently. Then, just when I thought things could get no worse, they did. There came a time when Ed would simply not come home at all some nights.

Life with him became more and more unbearable . . . and frightening. One night, I awoke from a sound sleep to find Ed standing over me. He whispered, as though not wanting anyone else to hear, "Come here; I want to show you something."

I reluctantly got out of bed and followed him through the den and into the kitchen, which had several large windows in the breakfast area overlooking the back of our land. He stood back a little way from the windows, as if trying to keep someone from seeing him and pointed out into the dark backyard area. He asked, "Do you see that?"

"See what?" I asked.

"That man," he said, "See him? He looks like a ghost, doesn't he?"

The hair stood up on my arms. I said, "Ed you are scaring me."

He said, "Why? Don't you see him?"

I said, "No, stop! You are frightening me." After a few minutes it became obvious that Ed no longer "saw him" either. I know now that the drugs were causing Ed to hallucinate.

On another occasion, Ed saw a bright light in the distance through our woods. He was convinced (and had me convinced) that it was some strange unexplainable phenomenon. (Yes, insanity is contagious when you live with an addict long enough.) It was only after a neighbor came over to take a look (and after much embarrassment) that we agreed it was a light from another house in the distance. Needless to say, I still go to great lengths to hide every time I see that former neighbor.

My mother lived in a small cottage on our land. One day our oldest son came home from visiting her and said, "Mama, I think Granny is losing it."

"What do you mean?" I asked.

He said, "She told me she saw a large bird today in the woods and that it was very tall!"

"Are you kidding me?" I asked.

He said, "No Mama, she said the bird was as tall as me!"

Later that day, as I was driving to the little country store up the road, I was thinking of all the craziness going on in our lives. "Ghosts in the night . . . strange lights in the woods . . . birds tall as humans . . . oh my!" As I got out of my car and was walking into the store, I saw on the door a sign written in big letters: MISSING EMU – AWARD OFFERED IF FOUND. I burst out laughing and said, "Thank you, Lord, that at least Granny isn't crazy."

This chapter is written to try to help you see that living with and loving an addict can make the abnormal seem normal, when in fact, it is not normal at all. If you suspect that your loved one is an addict, you could be right. I am not saying every abnormal thing that happens constitutes addiction, because it does not. However, there are many clear signs of addiction that too often we see only in hindsight. Personality changes, lying, disappearing for periods of time, stolen money, missing property, and changes in appearance and sleep patterns are just some of the signs. If things are going on in your life with your loved one that you can no longer excuse or explain away, open your eyes and take a closer look. I wish I had done so sooner.

Whether you suspect someone you love is an addict, or you know for certain they are, I encourage you to remember there is always hope and help for the addict and hope and help for you. I encourage you to seek out a good Al-Anon group for yourself, so you can learn the steps of recovery and the coping skills Al-Anon teaches. We, as co-dependents, can become almost as sick as the addict. Al-Anon helps you understand that you can live a happy and content life regardless of your circumstances and in spite of all the drama caused by your loved one.

More than anything, I encourage you to put your faith in God, and trust that He will be your strength. That is a promise He makes to us. Cling to and claim that promise. Even though you may be living in chaos right now because of the addict or alcoholic in your life, you can find peace and contentment. If your world seems to be falling apart today, if every "normal" thing in your life has become "abnormal," trust in the one who tells us that He never changes. He is our alpha and omega, the beginning and the end. He is the same yesterday, today, and forever. If everything around you is changing, trust Him. Run to Him. Follow Him. He will never lead you wrong.

"The name of the LORD is a fortified tower; the righteous run to it and are safe" (Proverbs 18:10).

CHAPTER 5

Christmas Eve

Ed had been clean (again) for about six weeks, and with each passing day my faith in him grew stronger. Although he had only had a couple of short bouts of "clean" time, I wanted to believe that this time it was for real. I cautiously began to think the nightmare and chaos we had been living in were slowly, but surely, coming to an end.

It was Christmas Eve, 1992. I remember it was a sunny, beautiful day, but bitter cold. I'm not sure why I can remember certain minute things about a day so long ago, such as the weather, but I do. The Christmas decorations in the house were very minimal that year. Normally, at Christmastime our house would be decorated to the hilt inside and out, and our Christmas tree would be surrounded with lots of gifts, almost to a fault. This Christmas was different. The gifts were few. Our sons were all past the Santa Claus stage, and I knew them well enough to know that even though there were only a few gifts under the tree, it would not matter to them. I knew that they, like me, were just so grateful we were all together this Christmas.

Ed and I both were raised to know the true meaning of Christmas, and we made sure that we raised our boys to know that meaning, too. Although I wanted us to stay focused on the true meaning of Christmas, I have to admit I was also hoping this Christmas would go by very quickly. I was more than ready for the New Year to arrive. In my mind, I thought the New Year would bring a new beginning, a new start, a new hope. Regardless of what the next year would bring, I was still very grateful that 1992 was finally coming to an end.

There was not much excitement in our house that Christmas Eve. After lunch, I noticed Ed casually walking by the Christmas tree, as if he was checking out the small number of wrapped gifts underneath. After about his fourth trip by the tree, he finally mustered up the courage to tell me he had a little money and wanted to go to town and buy each of us a gift. I tried my best to talk him out of it. I assured him several times that we did not need or want anything, but he was insistent. I knew Ed was struggling with an enormous amount of guilt for things he had done and he wanted to do something for our Christmas, so eventually I gave in.

He had been gone a couple of hours when the haunting feeling that something was very wrong kept flooding over me. It was a feeling I knew all too well. I began to pray silently that the sun would not go down, because darkness was always the telltale sign that something terrible was happening if Ed was not home yet. Of course, it happened... dusk, and then the dreaded dark.

Though I was consumed with fear, I tried to hide it. I kept reassuring our sons that everything was fine and that their dad was probably just caught up with all the last minute shoppers or stuck in traffic, and he would be home just any minute. No matter what I said to them and no matter how calm I tried to act, I could tell they were not buying any of it. I was not sure exactly what they knew about their father, but some of their fears were the same as mine. However, in an effort to try to comfort me, they agreed with me that, yes, he would be home soon.

Eventually, one by one, they gave up and went to bed. I remained up, waiting and praying. With every little sound I would jump up and hurry to the side door, hoping it would be him coming home. Time and time again, it was not. Finally, around four o'clock on Christmas morning, I heard a soft knock on the front door. The front door was a door only visitors, salesmen and strangers used. I got out of the recliner and tiptoed across the floor, as though whoever it was could hear me walking. I peeked around the corner and down the foyer so I could see who it was through the glass on the front door. It was Ed. All I can say at this point is that if you have ever lived with or loved someone in active addiction, you will understand what I mean when I say a part of me was so grateful to God that Ed made it home alive, and the other part of me wanted to kill him.

Our children were always very early risers on Christmas morning and this Christmas was no exception. Very shortly after Ed got home, the boys were awake and coming downstairs. This year, they were coming down early, not to open a bunch of gifts, but to find out if their father had made it home. They never asked what time he got home, and I never told them. However, I am sure they noticed that he had the same clothes on when he left the night before. It was like the elephant in the room that none of us wanted to acknowledge aloud.

Opening presents was always a whirlwind event on Christmas morning. I always took my time wrapping each gift and then it would seem like in one big swoop, all of the gifts would be opened and bows and paper would be flying everywhere! The house would normally be filled with laughter and everyone would be rushing around to see what the other one got. There would be a lot of hugging and a lot of "ooohs" and "aaahs" going on.

This Christmas was totally different. It was as though we all moved in slow motion. One by one, the few gifts under the tree were passed to the boys and each opened theirs. It was customary that Ed and I wait until the children were finished opening their gifts and then we would exchange our gifts.

For the first time in over twenty-four years, Ed had no gift for me. It is not that I needed anything or even expected anything that morning, but the sadness of how much drugs had changed our lives hit hard, and it hurt deeply. It was just another sad reminder of how drug addiction had affected our family, not only on a very big level, but even on such a small level as a simple Christmas gift.

I remember handing Ed his gift from me. He hesitantly took it and just laid it beside him, too ashamed and too embarrassed to open it. "Go ahead." I said, "Open it." He picked it up and held it. Then, he carefully removed the bow. He removed the wrapping paper one piece of tape at a time and then slowly opened the box. He looked up at me, our eyes met, and we stared at each other for a moment. It was a Bible. He opened the Bible and read the words I had hand-written inside it three weeks earlier: "To my husband with love. Never give up. Remember that all things are possible with God."

"Jesus looked at them and said, 'With man this is impossible, but with God all things are possible'" (Matthew 19:26).

CHAPTER 6

The Test

*I*t is odd how sometimes the smallest details of a major event in your life stand out in your mind. For instance, I remember that the day I found out Ed was on drugs was the most beautiful day I have ever seen; and, when I say "ever," I mean "ever." It was a fall day, and the sky was the clearest blue I have ever seen. The sun was so bright, the temperature was perfect, and the leaves were colors only God can paint. Yet, to me it was one of the darkest days of my life.

It was around lunchtime and I was sitting on the porch swing of our home, thinking about how our lives and marriage were unraveling in front of me. I had taken a sick day from work. I worked for a very busy divorce attorney. However, that particular morning I could not handle my own problems and heartache, so I knew I could not handle the problems and heartaches of others.

Life as I knew it with Ed had all but ended. Our relationship was extremely strained, at best, and I felt as if I had been living in a fog for a long time. It had been months and months since I had any clear direction on what to do, but when I awoke that morning, I knew for certain that day would be the day I would find out for sure if Ed was on drugs.

Oh, there had been a few times when in the heat of the moment as Ed and I would be "discussing" our dire financial problems or "discussing" Ed's erratic behavior, I would ask him if he was on drugs. Of course, each time I asked, he vehemently denied it. On one occasion, I asked him if he would take a urine test, and to my amazement, he agreed. However, since he "agreed," I never followed through with the test because I felt sure he would never agree to the drug test if he was really on drugs. Boy, if I only knew then what I know now!

Weeks later, I called his bluff and asked him again to take a drug test. After a short while, he returned holding a small bottle with what appeared to have urine in it. When he handed it to me, he had a look on his face that seemed to say to me, "If you don't believe or trust your husband, then go ahead, have it tested." So, what did I do? I poured it out. On this fall day, however, things would be different. I was determined if I could find Ed, I was going to get a urine sample.

I'm sorry if all this urine talk is disgusting; however, that's just where the water met the wheel that day. I was desperate. I felt I was losing my mind, and I had to know for sure whether or not Ed was using drugs.

I took a deep breath, said one more prayer, then got off the porch swing and went inside to the kitchen. I needed just the right thing. What could I use? What will work? I opened the cabinet door under the kitchen sink, and there it was. It was perfect—a Mason jar, complete with lid. It was just what I needed for "the sample."

During this time, Ed was very deep into his addiction, so I knew my chances of finding him were slim to none . . . and much closer to none. I knew that Ed and his work crew were doing renovations in an old abandoned warehouse down-town. However, I also knew Ed seldom showed up for work anymore. The warehouse was about thirty minutes from our home, so I grabbed the jar and headed to town.

I parked my car across the street from the old warehouse. As I walked toward it, I saw several different doors. I had no idea which door entered what part of the building. As I got closer, I just randomly picked a door and headed toward it. Right before I reached to open the door, it opened from the inside and there stood Ed. He was leaving. Had I been only a minute later, I would have missed him. There is no doubt in my mind that God intervened for me on that day.

When Ed opened the door, we were both stunned. To this day, I don't know who was more shocked—me, because I had actually found him, or him, because I was standing there in front of him... with a Mason jar in my hand.

It quickly became very clear to him why I was there. I said to him, "Ed, I have to know for sure, and I have to know today." I was not surprised when he agreed to the test, because he had agreed many times before; however, he was very surprised when I handed him the jar. He knew I was not bluffing this time.

I followed him toward the shabby bathroom in the old building, wondering if at any minute he would make a break for it and run. I stayed close. There was no way he was going in there alone or getting out of my sight. Afterward, nothing was said. I simply took the jar, turned around, and never looked back at him. I got in my car and drove away. My heart was pounding. I could not believe I had actually done this. At first, I felt so proud of myself, like I had really accomplished something. This would be the day that I would finally know the truth. Then fear suddenly overtook me. The truth? Could I even handle the truth?

As I was driving down the road, I came very close to pulling over to the edge and throwing the jar out. As strange as it sounds, I felt guilty, like I was the one who had done something wrong by asking Ed for the sample. It felt at some point in time, I had taken a marriage vow that said, "I will trust Ed for the rest of my life, no matter what." But the truth is, I was scared to death to find out the truth.

I took the jar to a friend of mine who worked for a lab. She had agreed to do the test for me under an anonymous name. I went home and sat with the telephone in my hand and waited for her to call with the verdict. I remember thinking to myself when the phone finally rang, "Just don't answer it and you won't know." Finally, I picked it up. "Barbara?" my friend asked. It was almost a whisper, and her tone of voice was the kind you use when you are delivering the worst kind of news to someone. "It's positive for cocaine."

If my life depended on it, I could not tell you anything else that was said between us. But I remember when I hung up, I put my face in my hands and cried, "Oh God, please help us."

The next few days were a blur. Ed was not home much, and the times I did talk to him, he continued to deny he was on drugs and tried to assure me the test was wrong or a "false positive." Trust me when I tell you that if an addict's lips are moving, he or she is lying. Ed's addiction only grew worse and so did the fate of our marriage and our livelihood.

I was at a loss at what to do; however, more than anything else, I wanted to get him help. I immediately began calling around and talking to various drug treatment facilities to find out what I needed to do to get Ed admitted for treatment. Each time, the person obtaining the information from me would ask me, "What kind of drug is he on?" Every time I would say the word "cocaine," I felt as though someone else was speaking that word about someone else other than Ed. The whole thing just seemed too unbelievable to me.

I remember one man in the admittance office telling me, "If he is on cocaine, the chances of him coming off of that drug are almost impossible." He said, "Treatment for cocaine is seldom successful." He had no words of encouragement at all. Years later, I realized neither that man, nor I, had factored into the equation the awesome power of God . . . a God who can change people and heal people. A God who loves to take our messes and make us messengers. A God who, if we do what we can, He will do what we can't.

A friend of mine recently shared a verse with me from Exodus 20:21 that says, " . . . and Moses went into the darkness, where God was." Where God was? The darkness? Before reading that verse, I never thought about God being in the darkness. I know God was with me on that fall day many years ago when I found out about Ed's addiction to cocaine, because He showed up in everything around me... in the blue of the sky, the brightness of the sun, and the colors of the leaves. I know now that on that fall day when my world seemed so hopeless and I could not see the light at the end of the tunnel, God was there with me in the darkness.

Throughout our marriage, Ed and I have always been playful. We often love to scare each other. Well, actually, Ed loves it much more than me. He thinks it is funny to jump out at me when I least expected it and yell, "BOO!" Sometimes I've walked into a dark room at home and although I couldn't see Ed, I would immediately know he was hiding in the room and just waiting for the right minute to scare me. I would always stop dead in my tracks and I would be very still, listening to hear any movement. Even though I could not see him in the darkness and even though I could not hear him in the darkness, I knew he was there . . . because I could just "feel" him.

Are you in the darkness today? Have you lost your direction and can't see your way out? Do you feel hopeless? Are you afraid? Believe me, you are not alone. I have been there. But, no matter what darkness you are going through, remember this: We serve a mighty and powerful God who is never afraid of the dark. Not only is He not afraid of the dark, He is in the darkness with you, and He will lead you out. I know, because He led me out.

Maybe you can't see Him, and maybe you can't hear Him; but be very still. . . can't you feel Him?

"Be still, and know that I am God" (Psalm 46:10).

CHAPTER 7

The Intervention

$\mathcal{B}$ y Webster's definition, "intervention" is defined as "(1) the act of intervening; (2) any interference in the affairs of another." However, having personally participated in an intervention, I think it would be better described as the "deepest form of heartfelt pleading that a person can possibly do."

You feel as if you are standing on the shore and throwing a lifeline to someone who is drowning, someone you love with all your heart, and begging him or her to grab hold of the rope. All the while, you know and must be resolved to the fact that if they do not grab the rope, they will drown right before your very eyes.

I planned many interventions for Ed. The problem was, he never showed up for any of them. At this point, Ed's addiction was full-blown. He was running full-throttle, and he was seldom home. I had come to learn that if I did not give up, I would eventually be able to corner Ed; and the time finally came when we caught up with him. Many of our close family members were there for the intervention. We gathered at our home and walked into the den area where we found Ed passed out in the recliner.

We all stood around Ed ready to "start" the intervention when he suddenly opened his eyes. I am not sure who was more startled, him or us. The truth is, none of us there had ever been through or participated in an intervention. We had no professional intervener there to guide us. We had not been through any intervention 101 classes or read any books on intervention. All we knew was someone we loved with all our hearts was dying due to drug addiction, and we could not and would not willingly sit back and allow it or enable him to do so any longer.

I can't help but laugh a bit at Ed's recollection of that evening. Years later, after Ed was clean and sober, I heard him talking to a friend of ours about the intervention. He said, "When I woke up and saw all of those people standing around me, I thought I had blacked out and woke up at a family reunion."

During our intervention, each of us begged, pleaded and cried, trying our best to convince Ed he had a serious problem and needed help. Our main goal was to convince him to go into drug treatment. The consequences for him not going into treatment would be he would have to leave our home, leave his children, and leave me.

The love shown for Ed that evening was overwhelming. Not one person, woman or man, held back their emotions or their tears. I remember wrapping my arms around Ed and begging him, with every ounce of strength left in me, to go into treatment. He refused.

When it was all said and done that night and it had become very obvious that our attempts at intervention had failed, my brother told Ed, "If you don't go into treatment right now, you are going to have to leave and not come back home, because there is no way that Barbara can take any more of this." My heart broke as Ed chose to leave.

Did Ed really want to quit drugs? I believe yes, with every fiber of his being he wanted to stop. However, there comes a time when an addict uses drugs for so long that he eventually uses against his own will. Addiction is like a vice-grip. Often, the addict truly believes that he or she can break free of the drugs and stop using any time they get ready. They live in denial. Ed was in denial. He tried to convince us he did not really have a problem and that even if he "did" have a problem, it was something he could fix on his own. Satan is the father of all lies, and he loves to keep us believing lies and living in denial.

Letting go of Ed that night was the hardest thing I have ever had to do. When he left our home, he left with only one small suitcase. He truly had no place to go, no place to live, and no one to live with; however, somehow in his sick addicted mind, that seemed more appealing to him than not using drugs.

That night, my brother, with a very heavy heart, drove Ed to the old abandon building where Ed had been working. My brother and Ed love one another like blood brothers. This night, neither of them said a word to each other the whole way there. When they arrived at the old building, my brother made one last effort to convince Ed to go into treatment. He turned to Ed and said, "If you don't go into treatment and get help to get off the drugs, I never want to see you again."

My brother only recently told me about this conversation. He told me, "Of course I was lying about not wanting to see him, but I was trying everything I could to convince Ed to get help."

I asked, "What did Ed say when you told him that?"

My brother said, "He got out of the car to leave, but then turned around and reached his hand through the passenger window, and we gripped hands tight. We we're both crying, and he said, 'I promise you if I can't stop the drugs, you will never see me again.'" It broke my brother's heart.

Ed ended up living in that empty warehouse for many days. This is a man who, before drugs, was intelligent, wise, kind, honest, gainfully employed, a businessman and a churchgoer. He was someone's son, brother, friend, father and my husband. Drugs had reduced him to a thin, pale, shell of a man who would choose to live in a cold, empty, abandoned building alone rather than give up cocaine.

Today, there are many, many men and women, young and old, living in worse conditions...under bridges, in condemned shacks, old cars, and cardboard boxes due to their addictions. Recently, I saw a man standing on the street corner holding up the sign that read, "I will work for food." He could have been the poster child for how far down addiction can bring a person. He had everything he owned in a torn and tattered backpack. He was unshaven, had unwashed, long scraggly hair, bad teeth, empty eyes, and was dirty looking. If I could have smelled him from the inside of my car, I am sure the stench would have been overwhelming. I wondered to myself, "Is that the smell of sin? The smell of wrong choices? The smell of despair? The smell of hopelessness?" Then I thought, "Isn't that the very smell God sent His son to die for?"

I wondered if there was ever an intervention for that man. I wondered how many friends and family members cried, pleaded, and did their very best to convince him to get help. I thought about all the bridges that person had burned, all the relationships that person had destroyed, and all the hearts that person had broken. Maybe I didn't know that man's name, but I knew him. I wanted to intervene, to lift that person up to God. I prayed for him...praying for healing, praying for hope.

Is there someone you know and love who needs an intervention today? Do you need to take a stand for someone who cannot take a stand on their own? I thank God for all those who showed up for the intervention with Ed and for all those who prayed for us, encouraged us, helped us, and so willingly and so lovingly, stood in the gap for us. One week after Ed left that night, he called home and wanted to go into treatment. Are you standing in the gap for someone?

"I looked for a man among them who would build up the wall and stand before me in the gap on behalf of the land so I would not have to destroy it, but I found none" *(Ezekiel 22:30).*

CHAPTER 8

Rebab

I was so relieved when Ed finally agreed to go into a drug rehabilitation facility. At the time, I thought he was sincere about wanting to get help for his drug addiction, but I would later learn the only reason he went into treatment was to "save our marriage." He knew I was not going to let him come back home until he got help, and in my mind, rehab was the answer.

It was a twenty-eight day program. On day one, Ed was already breaking rules. Newcomers to the facility were not allowed any incoming or outgoing telephone calls for the first two weeks. Ed, however, sneaked out of his room the very first night, found a phone, and called home. To his shock, I had changed our home telephone number to an unpublished number. He could not believe that I would actually do such a thing. As I think back, I have to admit it was very much out of character for me, but I desperately needed a rest.

He was trying to call me to tell me he would never use drugs again (translation: "to manipulate me into letting him come home"), to tell me that he had changed (translation: "to manipulate me into letting him come home"), to tell me he could quit using on his own (translation: "to manipulate me into letting him come home") and to tell me how sorry he was for everything (translation: "to manipulate me into letting him come home"). Not only was changing our telephone number the best thing I did, but that first night he was in treatment was the best night's sleep I had in a very, very long time. I finally knew where Ed was, I finally knew he was safe, and I was finally not waiting up for him to come home.

After his first week in rehab, I learned that spouses were expected to participate in the rehabilitation program, too. There were certain days when I would attend sessions alone and there were times when Ed and I would attend family sessions together. I remember the first family session we attended; all I could do was cry. All of my emotions were so raw.

I was so thankful Ed was there in treatment, but I have to admit I was also a bit ticked that I had to participate in the treatment program with him. The truth is, I wanted a break from everything. I was physically and emotionally worn out by this time. All I wanted them to do was "fix" him. I wanted it to be like dropping a car off at the shop. I wanted to say, "Please, just fix it, and call me when it is ready to pick up." Needless to say, it was much more involved than that.

After Ed's in-patient treatment, Ed and I attended what they called the "aftercare program." The aftercare group met once a week on Wednesday evenings at six-thirty in a large meeting room. There were usually around fifty to sixty of us. The group was made up of recovering addicts, alcoholics, spouses, and/or significant others. The Wednesday night meeting was usually a speaker meeting, where a recovering addict or alcoholic with a lot of sobriety time would share their strength, hope and experience with others.

I would like to be able to say that by this point in Ed's recovery, things were good for us, but they were not. Ed had relapsed many times even after his stay in rehab. Although the durations of the relapses were shorter than in the beginning,

I was fast losing hope that Ed would ever fully recover from his addiction.

One Wednesday night, rather than having a speaker meeting, the group decided anyone who wanted to could go to the microphone and share some hope with the others. I didn't want to be there that night. In fact, I thought to myself, "Hope? What hope?" I did not think I could go on one more day. I was too tired, life seemed too hard, and bad things had been going on for way too long.

As I was sitting there wanting to go home and having a really good pity party on my own, an older black woman named Miss Addie, whom we all had grown to love, slowly rose from her chair and walked to the podium. She was a recovering alcoholic with a lot of sobriety time. She was one of the winners, one of the miracles. She was always there on Wednesday nights; not only for herself, but I believe she knew she had much to offer to those who were still struggling. She normally did not do a lot of talking in the meetings, but when she did speak, she was like E.F. Hutton—everybody stopped what they were doing to listen to her.

When she got to the podium, she reached with one hand and gently pulled the microphone closer to her so we could hear. With the other hand, she held up her pointer finger to indicate the number "one" and she simply said, "You can make it, if you do it *one* day at a time, with *Him*." As she said that, she pointed upward and put heavy emphasis on the word *Him*. Then, in the clearest, sweetest, most soulful a capella voice, she began to sing the following old gospel song:

Precious Lord, take my hand, lead me on, let me stand;

I am tired, I am weak, I am worn.

Through the storm, through the night, lead me on to the light.

Precious Lord, take my hand and lead me home.

When she finished singing, she smiled, looked out into the audience and said, "Some of you out there need to take hold of Jesus." I knew beyond a shadow of a doubt that if I did not "take hold of Jesus" and fully lean on Him and trust in Him, I was not going to make it through this nightmare that had become my life. I could no longer do this by myself. I was slowly sinking deeper and deeper into hopelessness and I did not have the strength to climb out on my own. I knew I needed to take the focus off all of the loss and hurt in my life and focus fully on Jesus. I knew in my heart that I could not do this without Him.

Ed and I remained in the aftercare program for years and years and at some point during that time, Ed got clean and sober. Looking back, I see so many good things that came from rehab and the aftercare program for both Ed and me. We discovered we were not alone in our struggles. We made friends with so many people whose friendships we still cherish to this day. And we came to believe that no matter what, there is always hope.

As I look back on those days in rehab and in early aftercare, I remember how neither Ed nor I wanted to be there. It's not that we did not desperately want help. We did. It was just that the battle before us seemed much too huge for us to win. His addiction to drugs and our deteriorating marriage seemed too insurmountable. Today, I am so grateful for that treatment facility and the rehabilitation program. Even though Ed went into treatment for the wrong reason and even though I went into it with a bad attitude, we hung in; and the rewards from those years in treatment and aftercare are numerous.

Tonight, I again read the story in the Bible of young David and the giant Philistine, Goliath. Though I have read this story many times before, tonight is the first time these words jumped out at me: "David said to Saul, 'Let no one lose heart on account of this Philistine.'" What? I read that again, " . . . let no one lose heart on account of this

Philistine." In other words, he is saying, "Don't let this giant cause you to lose hope." Wow. This made me think of all the times I had let the "giants" in my life cause me to lose hope.

The difference between David and me is that while I focused on the giant, David focused on God. I knew how big the giant was, and David knew how big God was. I wanted to run from my giant, and David ran toward his giant. I could never figure out how to win the battle against my giant, and David knew the battle was not his at all. The battle was the Lord's.

Is there a giant in your life today? Are you overwhelmed? Do you feel defeated? Whatever giant you may be confronting today, whether it is addiction, loving someone in active addiction, whether it is a dwindling bank account, mounting debt, unemployment, or a failing marriage, I encourage you to give your giant to God and let Him help you through it. Nothing is too big for Him.

"David said to Saul, 'Let no one lose heart on account of this Philistine. . . '" (I Samuel 17:32).

"All those gathered here will know that it is not by sword or spear that the Lord saves; for the battle is the Lord's, and he will give all you into our hands.

As the Philistine moved closer to attack him, David ran quickly toward the battle line to meet him. Reaching into his bag and taking out a stone, he slung it and struck the Philistine on the forehead. The stone sank into his forehead, and he fell facedown on the ground" (I Samuel 17: 47- 48).

CHAPTER 9

The House

We lost everything due to drugs, including our dream home. In fact, it was auctioned off on the courthouse square. I am at a loss to even explain how despairing I felt on that day. Words like distraught, terrified, and completely heartbroken don't even come close to describing the level of emotional anguish I was feeling.

We moved from our large home on many acres into a single-wide trailer on a rented lot. I was too devastated and too embarrassed to ask anyone to help me move, so I packed up our whole home by myself, except for one thing I left in a closet upstairs.

After the very last load was taken to the trailer, I returned to the house, laid down on the floor in the middle of the large empty den, and wept. Even though the house was being foreclosed on, I wanted to make sure it was perfectly clean. I wanted the next owner to love it as much as me. I wanted to leave a letter on the kitchen counter so the potential buyer would see it and read it. I wanted them to know this was more than just another foreclosed home for sale. I wanted them to know it was our home, my home. I wanted them to take care of it for me. I wanted to tell them how much it meant to me. I wanted them to know how much love and hard work went into drawing the plans, clearing the land, building the home, all the sweat equity we had in the home, and how excited we all were to finally move in. I wanted them to know that for many, many years this home was bursting at the seams with love.

I then mopped, vacuumed, cleaned mirrors, washed windows and dusted until everything was spotless. There was not a speck of dirt anywhere. The whole house was empty, except for one thing. No, I did not leave the letter, but I did leave something in the closet upstairs that I could not bring myself to take with me.

As I cleaned each room of the house, I thought of all the love, fun, laughter, and energy that once filled the house.

I thought of all the Christmases and Thanksgiving dinners we had in the house. My whole family would come to our home for Thanksgiving each year. I could almost hear all of us laughing and talking. I thought about all the basketball games played by our boys outside. I thought of all our cats, hamsters, goldfish, dogs and the ferret that over the years called this place home. I thought about all the four-wheeling and exploring our boys did in the woods. I especially thought about all of the long walks Ed and I often took hand in hand in the woods, dreaming about our future.

But now what? How does one start over at this point in life with nothing? No house, no money, no retirement, no savings. I wondered to myself if I should take what I left in the closet upstairs and sell it, but I didn't even want to look at it. Though it was valuable to me at one time, it meant nothing to me now. It was just one less thing for me to pack; one less thing for me to find a place for in the trailer; and, one less memory to try to forget.

Our first holiday in the trailer was Thanksgiving. Normally, we would have thirty or more people in our home for Thanksgiving. I did not want to have Thanksgiving that year at the trailer. The truth is, "thanksgiving" was not my strong suit at the time. I finally decided that regardless of the space (or lack thereof), we would, in fact, have Thanksgiving dinner at the trailer. I worried that people would not come, but everyone came. Even some that didn't normally come for Thanksgiving showed up. All of us were squeezed in every-where—at the kitchen table, on the couch, chairs, sitting on the floor, standing, and outside on the deck. But you know what? It really didn't matter. In fact, it was wonderful. It was a reminder to me that as long as your family and friends are together, it really isn't important how much room you have or where you live. We may have lost a house and our material things, but we had the love of our family and friends, and that is priceless.

For at least a year after we moved into the trailer, Ed was still using drugs. I spent many nights alone in the trailer, and I cried myself to sleep often. There came a time when Ed had been gone for about a week. I had not heard from him and had no clue where he was. It was the first time I did not go out into the night looking for Ed. Normally, I would go out and try to find him. I have been in places looking for Ed that I think even the police would fear to go. This night, however, was not the same. Rather than going out to look for Ed, I went some place different. I went to my knees and prayed.

I had prayed many times before, bringing my pleas before God and begging Him to help us. But this night as I prayed, I believe with all my heart the Holy Spirit interceded for me. I felt completely hopeless, broken and powerless. I was on my knees for what seemed like a very long time and when I finally got up, I was exhausted, yet overwhelmed with a sense of peace.

I did not have a feeling that Ed was going to get clean and sober and I did not have a feeling that our marriage was going to survive, or that our finances would improve. In fact, I did not even know how I would make the next trailer payment. But what I did know was God was in control. I knew at that moment "I" could not fix the situation, but *He* could.

Things did not change overnight. In fact, Ed and I lived in that trailer for almost six years. At first, we seemed to just go through the motions of trying to get through each day, trying to regain some semblance of our marriage and of our lives. It was during our time in the trailer that Ed finally was able to get clean and sober. It was also during the time we lived in the trailer that both Ed and I began to lean on God and grow closer to God.

Something very spiritual began to happen to us in that trailer, something you really can't put into words. But this I know for sure: God had our full attention, and we knew we could not make it without Him.

That trailer became a spiritual safe haven for us. We could hardly wait to get back to the trailer each day after work. It had truly become our home. We learned to live at a slower pace, and we learned to love simplicity.

It was during this time that Ed began the saying "just right." Whenever anyone asked Ed how he was doing, his response would always be, "Just right." From the outside looking in, I am sure things did not look just right. We no longer had money, the big home, nice cars, the *things* that too often make life seem just right; but, Ed had learned to be content, regardless of the circumstances, and because of that, to him everything was just right. He had that contentment like Paul in Philippians 4:11-13:

I am not saying this because I am in need, for I have learned to be content whatever the circumstances. I know what it is to be in need, and I know what it is to have plenty. I have learned the secret of being content in any and every situation, whether well fed or hungry, whether living in plenty or in want. I can do all this through him who gives me strength.

In a recent letter to his dad, our middle son wrote about how when he left for college, he left his large childhood home and when he returned for Thanksgiving, he came back to a small trailer. Life changed for all of us. He also wrote in his letter about how proud he was of his father for overcoming great obstacles, how much he loves his father, and what a great example his father is to him. Today, I am so thankful our sons watched us go through those most difficult times because they saw us come out so much better on the other side. I don't mean materially, but spiritually.

If you love or live with an addict, you will more than likely lose many material things. You may know someone going through this right now or you may be going through it. If I could say one thing to you, it would be, "Never lose hope." What you are going through right now could turn out to be one of the best things that ever happened to you. I urge you to lean on God to help you through the hard times; and when you are in the depths of despair and think you are all alone, I hope the following verses from Isaiah 43: 2–3 will comfort you as much as they did me:

*When you pass through the waters, I will be with you;
and when you pass through the rivers, they will not sweep
over you. When you walk through the fire, you will not be
burned, the flames will not set you ablaze. For I am the Lord,
your God, the Holy one of Israel, your Savior.*

Notice that He does not say "if" you pass through the
waters, but he says "when" you pass through the waters. We
will all face difficult times in life, but He is with us.

As they say, hindsight is always 20/20, and as I look
back, I see how God worked in our lives in so many ways.
One of Ed's favorite sayings is, *"When the gold is in the fire,
the refiner is not far from the furnace."* We were in the fire. I
know now that God, our refiner, was very close.

Looking back, I also see all the promises God kept during
that time. Promises like: He is close to the brokenhearted;
He is my strength when I am weak; He will never leave me
nor forsake me; He is my refuge. Our heavenly Father is also
a God of restoration. He restored my hope, restored my faith,
restored my family and restored my husband.

Today, I have regrets about the one thing I left in the
closet upstairs in the foreclosed home. It was my wedding
dress. At the time, it was just a sad reminder of broken vows
and of a marriage that I was sure could never be restored.

However, God, in his great mercy and unconditional love, had other plans for us. Thank you, Father.

"For this reason I kneel before the Father, from whom his whole family in heaven and on earth derives its name. I pray that out of his glorious riches he may strengthen you with power through his Spirit in your inner being, so that Christ may dwell in your hearts through faith. And I pray that you, being rooted and established in love, may have power together with all the saints to grasp how wide and long and high and deep is the love of Christ, and to know this love that surpasses knowledge that you may be filled to the measure of all the fullness of God" (Ephesians 3:14-19).

CHAPTER 10

I Came to Believe

I was completely blindsided by Ed's addiction. Never, ever, would I have imaged that drug addiction would have been one of the "for better or worse" vows that would test my love for my husband and my commitment to our marriage. When the minister said "in sickness and in health," I was thinking something more along the lines of the flu or the occasional stomach virus, but drug addiction? No way.

When you live with someone who is in active addiction, over time it can suck all of your emotional well-being right out of you. At times, sanity and rational thinking go right out the window. You get caught up somewhere between enormous sympathy for what the addict is going through and enormous anger because he or she is causing you to go through it too. If you are reading this book, chances are you have been there and you know exactly what I mean.

"Step Two" of the Twelve Steps of Recovery is, "I came to believe that a power greater than myself can restore me to sanity." This is not only one of my favorite steps, but also the one that I needed the most.

Today, my sanity has been restored. Well, for the most part. But I remember clearly when my sanity seemed just beyond my reach. Ed and I were traveling to North Carolina for our youngest son's wedding. It was December 30, 1999. The wedding was the following day, New Year's Eve. As we traveled up Interstate 85, we were listening to southern gospel music. It was a late winter night. I guess the cold, the rain, and the Gaithers, all grouped together set the stage for my emotions to run wild—and run wild they did!

For many years, I had been struggling with anger and resentment from all the hurt and damage caused by Ed's addiction. I had always been very good at camouflaging my anger and resentment, and I am sure my friends and family thought I was pretty amazing by the way I had so "easily forgiven" and "moved on." But, I knew differently. Most of the time, I was able to keep my anger in check, but from time to time it would boil to the top and overflow into sarcastic remarks and hateful comments to Ed. I wanted to remind him just how much he had hurt me and hurt our family. It was as though I wanted him to remember that all of our problems were his fault, or so it seemed. In my crazy mind at the time, I thought if I reminded him often enough of how much he had hurt me, he would never do anything to hurt me again. Sick thinking, I know.

As we drove up the interstate in the pouring rain, the tears were pouring down my face. I thought of every broken vow, of every night that Ed did not come home, of every lie, of every material thing we had lost, of every heartache and on and on and on. Satan loves to keep us focused on the past and each time Satan would remind me of the past, I would, of course, remind Ed.

Ed was unusually quiet this night. I am sure he must have been thinking, "She is NEVER going to get over this." Normally, he would always defuse the situation by reassuring me he would never, ever, hurt me again and that if he could, he would take away all the hurt. This night, however, was different. There was only silence on Ed's part.

As we drove along, I began to recall how I had wanted so badly for Ed to turn his life back over to Christ and to "prove" to me that he had changed. The truth is, Ed *had*, in fact, turned his life over to Christ, and he *had* indeed changed. The problem was that I was not changing. I was still stuck in the past and wallowing in misery and a lot of self-pity. I was still in that deep dark pit called "resentment." Max Lucado wrote in his book, *The Applause of Heaven*: "Resentment is when you let your hurt become hate. Resentment is when you allow what is eating you to eat you up. Resentment is when you poke, stoke, feed, and fan the fire, stirring the flames, and reliving the pain."

That is exactly what I was doing. No one poked, stoked, fed, fanned, stirred, or relived pain any better than I did. Believe me, I took the prize. What I really wanted Ed to do was to "undo" everything and to make it as though it never happened. I wanted him to do the impossible.

As he drove, it dawned on me that Ed was no longer the one damaging our relationship, but it was I. You see, when one stays angry and resentful for so long (regardless of whether they have a reason to be or not), the tide begins to shift, and eventually they become the one doing the damage to the relationship.

The more I thought about it, the more I became fearful and thought to myself, "What if Ed begins to give up on us? What if he begins to believe that no matter what he does, it is never going to be enough for me? How long will it be before my anger and unforgiving heart drive him away?" I knew if I did not change, it would be only a matter of time before Ed would be the one leaving me.

The day after our son's wedding was the first day of the new millennium. The world had not come to an end as some had predicted, and the computers and banks had not all crashed, as some had anticipated. I woke up praying that morning. I prayed that the first day of the new millennium would mark a new beginning for Ed and me. I desperately wanted to get rid of all the anger and distrust that were still eating away at me. I wanted to be "restored to my sanity." I prayed, "Lord, I need your help to change. I need you to remove this anger from my heart and to take away all the resentment. I cannot do it alone. Please, Lord, restore me."

On our way back to the hotel room after saying our good-byes to friends and family, Ed and I stopped by the drug store to pick up a few items. We were both very quiet. I was still thinking about it being the first day of 2000 and wanting this to be a new beginning for us. I wanted my sanity back and I wanted my joy back. I wanted us to be happy again. I prayed that God would show me how to "get back there again." And then, on aisle four in the CVS drug store in a little town in the middle of North Carolina, "I came to believe" that it was time for me to change.

As Ed stood there in the aisle of the store studying all the many choices of soap to buy, he reached for his final selection . . . Lever 2000! Lever 2000? All I could think of was "Leave Her 2000!" With so many choices of beautifully named soaps such as Ivory, Dove, and Irish Spring . . . he chooses Lever 2000? I thought, "Is this my sign, Lord? Are you telling me something here Lord?" I looked at Ed, and he immediately looked at me; and we did what only two "sane" adult people could do standing in the middle of a drugstore—we laughed until we cried.

It was there on January 1, 2000 that God began to restore me to sanity. He also began to restore my joy and my sense of humor. It was then that I began to start letting go of all the resentments.

There is a saying that "Insanity is doing the same thing over and over again and expecting different results." It is only when we try a different path that we will find our way out of that deep pit of resentment. In difficult times, it's often easy to lose your way, to become angry and to become resentful. As they say, you can either let your circumstances make you bitter or make you better.

Are you struggling today with anger or resentment? Are the circumstances in your life eating you alive? Have you lost your peace, lost your joy, lost your sanity? If so, I know what bondage you are in, but there is a way back. Christ is the way. He will guide you. Follow His lead . . . let Him be your compass.

"Jesus answered, "I am the way and the truth and the life. No one comes to the Father except through me" *(John 14:6).*

"But the fruit of the Spirit is love, joy, peace, patience, kindness, goodness, faithfulness, gentleness and self-control" (Galatians 5:22).

CHAPTER 11

Forgiveness

I am no expert on forgiveness, but one thing I know for sure is it is very hard. It's difficult enough to forgive a friend who has hurt you or a parent or a sibling, but when you are faced with having to forgive a spouse, to me, that carries forgiveness to a whole new level.

I have found that you trust someone until they give you reason not to trust them anymore. Before his addiction, I trusted Ed completely. Never would I have ever imaged he would become addicted to drugs, and never in a million years would I have ever imagined all the pain and damage that can come from drug addiction.

My forgiveness of Ed came very slowly. I wanted to forgive him, I needed to forgive him, and I tried my best to forgive him; but I just couldn't. I acted like I had, but I knew I had not, and Ed knew I had not. Part of me felt like to forgive too quickly would be letting him "off the hook" too soon. I felt that if I quickly forgave, it would somehow lessen or make light of all the heartache his addiction had caused.

I remember a friend telling me, "Just act like you have forgiven him," so I did. I kept telling myself, "As soon as the hurt goes away, I will 'really' forgive him." The truth is (and I found out the hard way) the hurt will never go away until you forgive the person who hurt you. Harboring anger and resentment is self-destructing. There is a saying, "Resentment is like drinking poison and expecting the other person to die." That is so true. If you want to be free from anger and resentment, you must forgive.

I wanted that true feeling of forgiving Ed. I wanted to see him as I did before his addiction and before all of the heartache caused by that, but I just didn't know how to do that anymore. I wanted to be able to look at Ed and see him before he had grown the horns and tail. Okay, maybe he didn't actually do that, but close.

I prayed a lot about forgiving Ed. I asked God to give me strength and to give me a forgiving heart. I often thought about the verse, "Blessed are the merciful, for they shall receive mercy." I thought of God's grace and unconditional love for me and of all the times God had forgiven me when I was so undeserving. It finally dawned on me one day that my forgiving Ed really didn't have anything to do with Ed. My forgiveness of Ed was between God and me, not Ed and me. Even though I may have wanted forgiveness to be an option, it was actually a commandment. When I finally accepted that forgiving Ed meant obeying God, forgiving Ed became easier. I am not saying it happened overnight, because it did not, but eventually it did happen.

Years after Ed had been clean and sober, we were at home in our den. It was late one evening and Ed had fallen asleep in his recliner. Earlier that week, in a class that I was in at church, the teacher had given each woman the task of writing a poem about her husband. As I looked at Ed asleep in the chair, the following words just came to me:

We met when I was 12 years old, much too young
to know just where our lives would lead us, or
how deep our love would grow.

I married him at 17, much too young I'm sure; and, never guessing of the trials our marriage would endure.

Now, I could tell you of the hard times and things too sad to bear; but I want to tell you of a new and changed man, with whom my life I share.

He's a man with many titles: husband, sweetheart, friend, dad, and now Paw Paw; and, when I ponder just how far he's come, I have to stand in awe.

I've watched him grow so strong in faith, he's such a Godly man today, and I've never seen him stand so tall as when he kneels to pray.

And the words he prays are from his heart. A grateful man is he, for he knows through prayer, and by the grace of God, from drugs he's been set free.

Oh, he loves to help and he loves to give to those with less that he,

but he doesn't like to talk about it, he just does it anonymously.

And if you ever see a penny on the ground and it's heads up, well, chances are he left it there, so you would have good luck.

He loves wearing shorts and golf's his sport. He loves hot peppers and he loves tractors. He loves his sons, their wives and his grandchildren's laughter.

He loves pasta with cheese, and he loves me. He loves all children, but his favorites are Anna, Savannah, Luke and Brooklyn.

Now when he sees you, he will hug you, woman, man or child; and he'll tell you that he loves you, and he does so with a smile.

And, when he tells you that he loves you, those aren't just words to him, for he wants you to know how much he cares, should you never meet again.

He's been my man for almost thirty years, and down many roads we've trod, but most of all, I'm proud to say, he is now a man of God.

When I finished writing that poem, I gently shook Ed to wake him and told him I wanted to read something to him.

I sat on the floor next to him and I read the poem. When I finished reading it, I looked up at him and saw tears in his eyes. He told me that for the first time, he felt as though I had finally forgiven him.

As I was driving today in my car and listening to our local faith radio channel, I heard the story of a racecar driver who chose the number "490" for his race car. The numbers were largely painted on both sides of his car. Underneath the number "490" it boldly said, "SEVENTY TIMES SEVEN." The person telling the story about the race car driver said that the racetrack was not normally a place where you would hear someone testifying about their faith; however, this race car driver used his car and these numbers as an opportunity to share his faith every chance he got. Person after person would ask the driver, "What does the 'seventy times seven' mean?" That always opened the door for him to tell the Bible story in the book of Matthew about forgiveness:

Then Peter came to Him and said, 'Lord, how often shall my brother sin against me, and I forgive him? Up to seven times?' Jesus said to him, 'I do not say to you, up to seven times, but up to seventy times seven' (Matthew 18:21-22, New King James).

Take it from someone who knows—an unforgiving heart hurts everyone. No one wins. Are you struggling with an unforgiving heart today? Are resentment and anger robbing you of joy? Does your unwillingness to forgive have you in bondage? If so, don't let Satan keep you captive one more minute. Break free and forgive . . . seventy times seven.

"For if you forgive men when they sin against you, your heavenly Father will also forgive you. But if you do not forgive men their sins, your Father will not forgive your sins" (Matthew 6:14-15).

CHAPTER 12

Isolation and Denial

Some people who encounter hard times or emotional trauma seek help from others. Some seek help from friends and family and some seek out professionals. However, there are some people who, when they encounter hard times or emotional struggles, retreat and isolate themselves. That would describe me. Well, that would describe me back when Ed was in active addiction.

I wanted to hide and to avoid people. There were some people who knew about Ed's addiction and some people who only suspected it. I didn't want to talk with any of them. I was afraid that those who suspected Ed was on drugs would ask me questions, trying to confirm whether it was true or not. And I was afraid to talk with those who knew for sure that Ed was on drugs, for fear that they would tell me things I did not already know and certainly did not want to find out. I also avoided people because there comes a time when you are just worn out from even thinking about what's going on in your life, much less actually talking about it. When I would talk about things, it seemed to give them "life." Yet when I isolated myself, stayed quiet and avoided people, it felt like I was more in control. Personally, I don't think *some* isolation in and of itself is harmful... unless of course you stay there. I eventually came out.

Denial, on the other hand, is a very dangerous place to dwell for long. Denial is when, even though deep down inside you suspect what is really going on, that powerful emotion called fear causes you to believe lies, look the other way, justify things, make excuses for and cover up.

When I finally realized that I could no longer ignore the signs of addiction, I confided in and leaned on certain friends and family members who I knew were safe: those who I knew would not be judgmental, those who I knew loved both Ed and me unconditionally, and those who could help me look at things through different eyes. They were my strength, confidants, encouragers and prayer warriors. They prayed with me, cried with me, advised me and guided me when I could barely put one foot in front of the other.

I remember one evening I was neck deep in denial and waiting for Ed to get home from work, or so I thought it was work. It was another one of those many nights when he had called home and said he was running late getting back into town from a job. By this time in our ordeal, I knew something was seriously wrong, but I still could not bring myself to fully believe it was drugs. I sat with the phone in my hand that night, waiting anxiously for Ed to call and tell me what time he would be home.

Finally, around ten-thirty, the phone rang. I answered it before it could even finish the first ring. It was Ed. I asked, "Ed when are you coming home?" As soon as I asked, he acted as if we had a bad connection and no matter what I said, his response was always, "I can't hear you." I frantically went from room to room trying to get a "good connection," each time getting louder and louder as I asked, "CAN YOU HEAR ME NOW?" I felt like I was in a really bad cell phone commercial. I continued to ask, "Can you hear me now?" and "Are you coming home?" Before I knew it, I was screaming at the top of my lungs, trying my best to get him to hear me.

I happened to look up, and my precious son was walking toward me. I am sure I looked like some crazed woman screaming into the telephone. He gently pried my fingers off the telephone, while softly saying, "Mama, daddy can hear you and he is not coming home." Then he hung up the phone and turned and went back into his room. It was like he jolted me back to reality. I stood there thinking how I had "lost it" and how easy it is to get caught up in the insanity of someone's addiction. That night, Ed's addiction not only controlled him, but it controlled me too.

Even after I came out of denial and admitted to myself that Ed had a drug problem, I still went to great lengths to try to hide Ed's addiction from our sons. I thought I was doing the right thing and that I was "protecting" them . . . and him. The two oldest children found out first. I remember the day I told our youngest son about his father's addiction. My heart was so heavy. It is not the kind of news you ever want to have to tell a child. However, when I told him, he acted almost relieved. Don't misunderstand, he was scared for his father and very sad, yet he told me that he felt like the missing piece of puzzle was finally found. He had watched his father change so drastically, yet he did not understand why. He saw his dad go from a kind, loving, fun, attentive father to almost a stranger. I will never forget him telling me, "At least I know now it is drugs causing him to act this way, because I was afraid Dad had stopped loving us."

I've said it before, and I will say it again: Satan loves to keep us isolated and to keep us in denial. Do you know why? Because then he is in control. When we are withdrawn, refusing to acknowledge our circumstances and paralyzed with fear, how can we be effective for God? How can we move forward? The longer we deny a loved one has a drug or alcohol problem, the longer the problem will continue. Sticking your head in the sand will not make the problem disappear, and condoning bad behavior only reinforces bad behavior.

Satan loves to keep us afraid—afraid of finding out the truth, afraid of the unknown, afraid of others finding out, afraid of confronting the addict, afraid of change and afraid of the future. Fear causes you to play out in your mind the worst-case scenario of every situation. God knows how susceptible we humans are to fear. I believe that's why the most repeated command in the Bible is "fear not." Our Heavenly Father does not want us to live in fear. He wants us to walk in faith.

Several years ago, I met a woman in a recovery class I attend, whom I will call Ann. Ann had custody of her young grandson because her daughter was an active drug user. Ann shared with the class about her daughter's addiction and struggles caused by addiction. In fact, her daughter was so addicted to drugs that she went from a beautiful, intelligent businesswoman who once owned her own company to a street prostitute. She literally sold herself for drugs. She had been beaten up several times by different "Johns" and pimps. She suffered many broken bones, knocked-out teeth and had been arrested numerous times.

Whenever Ann spoke of her daughter, I was always amazed and fascinated by the inner sense of peace she seemed to have, even in spite of her circumstances. The last time I saw Ann, I asked her about her daughter, and she said her daughter had been missing for months. They had not been able to find her and were not even sure if she was dead or alive.

I asked Ann, "How is it that you can get up each morning and go through each day, knowing that your daughter is missing and watching your grandson grow up without his mother?"

She looked at me square in the eyes, smiled and said, "Because I walk by faith, and not by sight."

That's the kind of faith I want. That's the kind of faith I strive to have.

Are you living in denial about someone you love? Are you living with blinders on so that you don't have to see the truth? Do you see the truth, but then look the other way so that you don't have to face the hurt? Trust me when I say that just because we deny there is a drug or alcohol problem, the problem does not cease to exist. Don't be afraid to face the truth. Are you isolating? Find someone safe, someone you trust to give you Godly advice. Are you afraid that there is no hope for your situation? Remember that there is always hope.

Take my hand, and let's walk by faith and not by sight.

"Now faith is being sure of what we hoped for, and certain of what we do not see" (Hebrews 11:1).

" . . . for we walk by faith, not by sight"
(II Corinthians 5:7).

CHAPTER 13

Don't Love Me to Death

I cannot begin to tell you all the things I did "in the name of love" to try to help Ed through his addiction. I wanted to help him because I loved him and because he was my husband, my best friend, my partner and the father of our children, but mostly because I remembered what a good man he was when he was clean and sober.

I learned the hard way that there is a very fine line between "helping" and "enabling" an addict. It is a very dangerous line and if you cross it too many times, you begin to hurt your loved one instead of helping him. Generally speaking, to help someone is to do something for that person which they are not capable of doing on their own. When you enable someone, you do something for that person that not only they are *capable* of doing on their own, but that they also *should* be doing on their own.

Some examples of enabling would be rescuing the addict over and over again, continually paying his bills because he will not work or is currently incapable of keeping a job, giving him money, bailing him out of jail, providing a free place to live, never letting him face the consequences of his own addictive behavior; and, always making excuses for him. All of these things came to my mind very quickly because I have done most of them. I think the reason I did some of these things was because I simply did not know what else to do and felt I had to be doing something. However, I can say first-hand and with great certainty . . . enabling does not work.

I will never forget sitting in our recovery class at church one evening. On that particular night, the topic was on enabling. There was a young man in his twenties in the class that night for the first time. I could tell that he was listening very intently to what others were saying about enabling. He finally summoned the courage to speak up, and this is what he said: "My mom and dad are good people, and they love me very much. They have done everything they can possibly do to try to help me through my addiction, but they have almost loved me to death." He went on to talk about all the times they rescued him, made excuses for him and "saved" him from every consequence of his addiction.

They, like me, did all of this in the name of love, but what they did not understand was they were "loving him to death." As long as we make life easy for the active addict, what incentive do they have to change?

Addiction is not only very serious, it can also be deadly. My husband came close to dying on drugs and during the past nineteen years that he has been in recovery, we personally know nineteen people who sadly did not live through their addiction. Most of them were friends, some were good friends, and one was family. Some died accidentally and some died intentionally. They died from overdoses, car wrecks, gunshot wounds, alcohol poisoning, cirrhosis of the liver, heart attacks, murder and pure hopelessness. The one murdered was a dear friend who was shot in the back while trying to escape her alcoholic husband, who then turned the gun on himself.

It's hard to bring up such horrible memories, and I don't do so lightly or for the shock factor. I bring it up because the truth is, addiction can be deadly and we need to treat it that way. Too many people we know and love are dying from it.

I love the story in the Bible of the prodigal son, and tonight I read these verses again:

Jesus continued: There was a man who had two sons. The younger one said to his father, "Father, give me my share of the estate." So he divided his property between them.

Not long after that, the younger son got together all he had, set off for a distant country and there squandered his wealth in wild living. After he had spent everything, there was a severe famine in that whole country, and he began to be in need. So he went and hired himself out to a citizen of that country, who sent him to his fields to feed pigs. He longed to fill his stomach with the pods that the pigs were eating, but no one gave him anything.

When he came to his senses, he said, "How many of my father's hired servants have food to spare, and here I am starving to death! I will set out and go back to my father and say to him: Father, I have sinned against heaven and against you. I am no longer worthy to be called your son; make me like one of your hired servants." So he got up and went to his father.

But while he was still a long way off, his father saw him and was filled with compassion for him; he ran to his son, threw his arms around him and kissed him.

The son said to him, "Father, I have sinned against heaven and against you. I am no longer worthy to be called your son."

But the father said to his servants, "Quick! Bring the best robe and put it on him. Put a ring on his finger and sandals on his feet. Bring the fattened calf and kill it. Let's have a feast and celebrate. For this son of mine was dead and is alive again; he was lost and now is found." So they began to celebrate (Luke 15:11-24).

Most of us could probably say there have been times or seasons in our lives when we were prodigal sons or prodigal daughters. But tonight as I finished reading this story again, I noticed all the many similar traits between an addict and the prodigal son. I also noticed for the first time all the things the father did and did not do.

So many addicts, like the prodigal son, go off to a "distant country" and squander their wealth on "wild living." However, the father, unlike me, did not go into the distant land, or the bars, or drive the streets at night to look for his loved one to try to bring him home. Sometimes we, as co-dependents and enablers, spend a lot of time "checking up on," following, calling, and questioning our addicts or alcoholics about their whereabouts, actions, money, et cetera. We become consumed with needing to know every move they make. We begin to think we are pretty skilled detectives and private eyes (sometimes bordering on stalking) just so that we can "prove" to ourselves and to our loved one that we *know* they are not telling us the truth. Martha, a dear friend and addiction counselor, once told me, "You don't have to prove a lie. You know he is lying, he knows he is lying, and God knows he is lying." When that finally sunk in, it was liberating.

When the prodigal son had "spent everything and began to be in need," the father did not send him money or pay his bills. When the prodigal son was hungry and no one would give him anything to eat, the father did not take him food or give him a Winn-Dixie gift card.

Nowhere do we read where the father in any way "enabled" the son. In fact, when the prodigal son hit "rock bottom" and had no one to undo the consequences of his actions, what did he do? He "came to his senses" and returned home to his father.

What did the father do? He waited and watched daily for his son. He remained compassionate, and he never gave up hope. And when his son returned home, he celebrated. Can't you just see the father running towards the son? What a beautiful picture.

The Father is also waiting and watching for our prodigal sons, daughters, and spouses. As long as we are there to pick up the pieces of the addict's destruction, ease the pain, and fix the problems, will he or she ever get clean and sober? I love Job 36: 15-16: "But those who suffer, He delivers in their suffering. He speaks to them in their affliction; He is wooing you from the jaws of distress."

God knows that when we are suffering, we are more apt to be open to his wooing. Our loved ones may never lean on God, unless we stop letting them always lean on us.

There is a saying in recovery: "Let go and let God." It's about releasing that white-knuckle grip you have on someone and praying that, like the prodigal son, he will "come to his senses" and return home. Some people call it "tough love," and it is exactly that . . . tough. At times, it was the hardest thing I've ever done. I am certainly not saying that I mastered it, but I am a true believer in it.

If you are dealing with an addict or alcoholic, I encourage you to set your boundaries. Draw a line in the sand, and let them know what you will and will not tolerate, what is acceptable and what is not acceptable. I was good at setting boundaries, but at times I moved my boundary lines when I felt pressured. Don't move your boundary lines.

Are you enabling someone today? Are you trying to "fix" someone, even though it is not within your power to change them? Do you keep moving your boundary lines? Is there someone in your life whom you need to "let go" and give to God? It is my prayer that all of us will do a lot less enabling and a whole lot more celebrating. The life of someone we love may just depend on it.

"But the father said to his servants, 'Quick! Bring the best robe and put it on him. Put a ring on his finger and sandals on his feet. Bring the fattened calf and kill it. Let's have a feast and celebrate. For this son of mine was dead and is alive again; he was lost and is found.' So they began to celebrate" (Luke 15:22-24).

CHAPTER 14

Rosie

*M*ost addicts I personally know have what they call "triggers." A trigger is something that causes them to think about using drugs again or causes them to relapse. For some addicts, a trigger could be running into another addict they used with, or driving past an area where they once bought drugs. Ed always paid for his drugs with twenty-dollar bills, so for Ed, the trigger was a twenty-dollar bill.

Early in Ed's recovery, having a twenty-dollar bill in his pocket caused him to stumble and relapse many times. Even after Ed got clean, there was a very long period of time that he would not allow a twenty-dollar bill to be in his possession. If a cashier or bank teller was giving Ed money or change back, he would always ask for ones, fives, or tens, but never twenties. I tell you this so in reading this chapter, you can fully understand the effect a twenty-dollar bill once had on Ed.

Ed is not the kind of person who talks about himself. If anything, you have to pull information out of him; but I will share one of my favorite stories about him.

Ed sells farm equipment for a living, so he often travels backcountry roads. One day he stopped at a country store to get a cola and some crackers. While he was standing in line to pay, he noticed an elderly woman in front of him was a little short in having enough money to pay for the groceries she was purchasing. All Ed had on him was a fifty-dollar bill that he had stuck back in his wallet for an "emergency." Ed offered to pay the few dollars she was short and she accepted.

After Ed made his purchase, he got back in his truck and left. As he pulled out of the parking lot, he noticed the same woman was walking down the country road in the hot sun, with grocery sacks in both arms. Ed pulled over and offered to give her a ride and she again accepted. She lived only a mile or so from the store, but much too far for someone at her age to be walking, especially in the summer heat.

As they rounded a curve in the narrow country road, she pointed to the little house on the left and Ed turned in. It was a very crude, small, one-room shack. The front yard was just dirt, no grass, and the porch steps were so old and dilapidated that they had separated some from the house. Ed helped her out of the truck with her groceries. He knew she had no money, so he reached in his pocket and pulled out the change he received from the country store and in his hand was a twenty-dollar bill. When he saw it was a twenty, he hesitated a minute, then quickly handed her the twenty-dollar bill. What was a "trigger" to Ed turned out to be a blessing to someone else that day. That was the beginning of a special friendship between the two of them that lasted years.

The next time Ed was in her area, he made it a point to stop by to check on her and to visit a while. Later, as Ed was walking across the dirt yard to his truck to leave, she asked, "Who are you?" Ed realized that they had never even asked one another's name.

He said, "My name is Ed."

She said, "Who sent you here?"

As he continued to walk away, he smiled, pointed up towards heaven, and simply said, "A friend of mine sent me."

As he was getting in his truck, he heard her say, "He's my friend, too."

Over the next few years, Ed visited with her, prayed for her and often took her things . . . sometimes money, sometimes groceries. One day he asked me if I had any clothes that he could take to someone in need, so I gathered up some clothes. At the time, I did not know who the clothes were for.

Her name was Rosie Ferguson. She was a thin woman with black skin and silver hair. She had one missing front tooth and she smiled the whole time she was talking with you. She was probably in her late seventies. The way I learned about Rosie was one Saturday, Ed and I were just out riding around and he took me by her home to meet her. When we pulled up in her yard, she came hurrying out of the little shack, waving and smiling big. She was at the truck before we could even get out of it. She quickly walked up to Ed's side of the truck and placed her hand on his arm as she looked in the truck window to see who Ed had with him. When Ed introduced us, she smiled the biggest smile and said, "Thank you, honey, for the clothes."

Ed saw Rosie many times over the years. However, the day came when Ed went by her home to see her, and a young man came out to his truck when he pulled into the yard. It was her grandson. He told Ed that his grandmother had passed away just that morning. She had never complained to Ed and unbeknown to him, she had been fighting cancer for the past year. She never told Ed she was sick and because she was always smiling and always so happy to see Ed, he never knew anything was wrong.

We learned from her obituary that she had eight children and eighteen grandchildren. Ed and I attended her viewing at a small country church. The church was packed and if I had to guess, probably most of them were family. Ed and I were the only white people there. I stood beside Ed at her casket and could tell his heart was heavy as he looked at Rosie.

When we turned to leave, I saw a little girl tug on her father's pants leg and point to Ed. I heard her whisper, "Who is that white man?"

Her father looked down at her and softly said, "He is Granny's friend."

The story really doesn't stop here. About a year after Rosie passed away, Ed met a friend and neighbor of hers. One day Ed stopped by to visit the neighbor who, like Rosie, was an elderly woman and lived in similar conditions as Rosie. When Ed got up to leave, he gave her a twenty-dollar bill. The next time he saw her, she asked, "Do you know what I did with that money you gave me?"

Ed said, "No, what?"

She smiled and said, "I bought some flowers for Rosie's grave."

I love this story because it makes me think about how God often intervenes for us and puts people in our paths and in our lives just at the right time and just when we need them the most. On that hot summer day when Ed first met Rosie, he was a recovering addict with a twenty-dollar bill in his pocket and striving to stay clean day by day. Rosie was an elderly woman with very little income, striving to make ends meet day by day. I do not think it was a coincidence that their paths crossed that day.

To me, Ed is the modern day Good Samaritan. He doesn't look the other way when he sees someone who needs help. Instead, he goes toward them. Some people are beaten up by life and some people are beaten up by the consequences of their own actions. Regardless of who or what caused the pain, as a good friend of ours always says, "There's a lot of hurting people out there."

Ed also reminds me of Barnabas in the Bible, whose name means "son of encouragement." He just has a way of mentoring others and encouraging others. People are often drawn to Ed because they know about his addiction and of his recovery. They see the changed man he is today and they truly want what he has.

I have many other stories about Ed helping others, encouraging others, mentoring others, and my favorite — baptizing others. A friend of ours recently sent Ed a card that says, "Only on judgment day will you ever know just how many lives you have changed."

That card pretty much sums up all my stories about Ed. Once addicted to cocaine, now an advocate for Christ.

"News of this reached the ears of the church at Jerusalem, and they sent Barnabas to Antioch. When he arrived and saw the evidence of the grace of God, he was glad and encouraged them all to remain true to the Lord with all their hearts. He was a good man, full of the Holy Spirit and faith, and a great number of people were brought to the Lord" (Acts 11:22-24).

CHAPTER 15

Storms

As I write this chapter, it is just a few days after the worst tornado outbreak ever in the state of Alabama. Many towns were devastated. The little town of Hackleburg, Alabama was completely destroyed. Tuscaloosa, Alabama was one of the hardest hit. Many people lost their properties, their homes—their lives. At this time, hundreds of people are still missing and places that were ravaged by the tornado look like war zones. The sadness and shock of it all is overwhelming. Yet, even in the midst of all of the heartache and loss, there are still remarkable stories of amazing survivals and most of all, stories of hope.

Two of our dearest friends, Bill and Norma, lived on Lake Martin, Alabama. During the early evening on the day of the tornados, Norma nervously watched The Weather Channel, carefully monitoring the tornado alerts. Their sons live near Birmingham, Alabama and on this evening, the Birmingham area was directly in the path of an F-4 tornado.

While Norma was on the telephone with one of her sons, he told her that a tornado alert has just gone out for Tallapoosa County, the county where Bill and Norma lived. Her son said, "Mama, you and Dad need to get to the basement quickly." Norma hung up the phone; however, before they could make it to the basement, they heard the freight train sound that accompanies a tornado. They realized there was no time to get into the basement, so they dashed into the bathroom. Norma laid down on the floor, Bill covered her with his body, and they prayed.

Rescuers were unable to reach Bill and Norma by land due to downed power lines, uprooted trees and debris from destroyed homes. Finally, after numerous hours of being trapped in a house that was barely standing and hardly recognizable as their home, rescuers (one of whom was their son) managed to get to them by boat. Though they lost their home and possessions, they had each other and were miraculously uninjured.

The next day, when Bill and Norma returned to see the damage to their home, they were shocked by the extent of the wreckage, yet amazed by what they saw in the bathroom where they took refuge. Though the roof was gone, windows were blown out, and the house was beyond repair, there in the bathroom where Bill and Norma had laid praying, the hand towel was still neatly folded on the vanity and the soap was still in the soap dish. There is no doubt that our heavenly Father was watching over them that night.

There will be times when we will go through storms in life. Some are created by Mother Nature, some are created by the ones we love, and some are created by us. I have never lost a home to Mother Nature, but I have lost a home due to drugs. Regardless of the type of storm, the loss can be devastating. But the good news is this: there is always hope. Just like those who survived the tornados created by Mother Nature, there are many, many who survive and overcome the storms of addiction.

I love the line in an old gospel song that says, "Sometimes He calms the storm, and sometimes He calms me." There have been times in my life when God has either calmed the storm or given me the strength to get through it. Aren't you grateful that no matter what kind of storms we go through, we know the one who controls the storm?

As I am sitting on my sofa tonight writing this chapter, Ed is sitting in his recliner talking on the phone to a man who is struggling with drug addiction. The man is telling Ed about all the hurt and destruction his addiction has caused his family. He is in the midst of a major storm that he has created himself. The man is tired, weary and on the brink of giving up. He feels hopeless. He does not believe that he will ever have his family back or get his life back to the way it was before drugs.

Ed listens to him and then tells him, "You are right. Your life won't ever be the same as it was before, but it can be *better* than it was before. In fact, it can be *just right.*" No one knows or believes that any more than Ed. Ed continues to talk to the man, continues to encourage him. What Ed is really doing is throwing a lifeline to someone who is drowning…to someone who desperately needs some hope.

Ed and I have been through other storms. One storm in particular, though it had nothing to do with Ed's recovery, brought back old feelings of fear, and at times I felt over-whelmed. One day I asked Ed if what we were going through made him afraid, and he said, "No, I have prayed about it and turned everything over to God." I, on the other hand, though I had prayed and prayed (and had my strong prayer warriors praying too), was often still filled with fear. Ed reminded me that fear and faith cannot walk hand in hand. It is not that I did not trust God to get us through this storm, because I did. It was just that I did not want to go through another storm.

One evening, I was sitting in the recovery class at church, trying to look normal, but on the inside I was really a mess. I looked at Ed sitting next to me. I studied his face and he looked so calm. He was presenting the lesson that night and when the class started, he walked to the microphone and said, "Life can change on a dime."

Without going into any specifics, he talked about being in a storm again. He said, "The difference between now and many years ago when I was in active addiction is that today I have a strong foundation." Today, his reaction was to pray continuously and to trust God. He talked of the Bible story in Matthew about building your house upon the rock so that when the storms of this life come (and they *will* come), you can stand firm and your house will not be destroyed.

The truth is, most of us are either going into a storm, in the middle of a storm, or coming out of a storm. The trick is to not lose your footing. Satan would love nothing more than for winds of adversities, heartaches and troubles to blow so hard in our lives that they knock us right off our foundation.

After the tornado outbreak in our area, the sale of storm shelters increased dramatically. I think about all the people who were fortunate enough to have storm shelters during the tornados. They were the lucky ones, the saved ones.

What about you? Are you in a storm now? Is your foundation strong? Are you like the drug-addicted man Ed is talking to tonight? Are you tired? Weary? Have you lost all hope and are you on the verge of giving up? Remember you have a lifeline. His name is Jesus. Grab hold. He can pull you from the wreckage. Put your faith in the one who rebukes the winds and calms the waves. Let Him be your refuge. Let Him be your storm shelter.

"As they sailed, He fell asleep. A squall came down on the lake, so that the boat was being swamped, and they were in great danger. The disciples went and woke him, saying, 'Master, Master, we're going to drown!' He

got up and rebuked the wind and the raging waters; the storm subsided, and all was calm. 'Where is your faith?' he asked his disciples. In fear and amazement they asked one another, 'Who is this? He commands even the winds and the water, and they obey him'" (Luke 8:23-25).

CHAPTER 16

PUSH

*H*ave there ever been times in your life when, no matter how close you tried to stay to God, you just felt spiritually dry? Divinely depleted? I had several "dry spells" during Ed's addiction when I just did not feel connected to God, times when I did not think God was hearing my prayers. However, once Ed got clean and sober, my spiritual life and my connection to God seemed to grow more and more with time.

Then, several years into Ed's sobriety, the "closeness" that I had been feeling towards God seemed to wane again. I could not understand it. I was doing the things I thought I needed to do, yet I continued to feel distance between God and me. I decided I would become very proactive. I prayed more, read my Bible more and joined a weekly ladies' Bible class. I was doing everything I could think of to get close to God again.

I had been attending my ladies' Bible class for about four weeks, trying my best to "feel spiritual" again. I was sitting on the fourth row of the class when the teacher announced that she wanted to do an experiment. She began looking around the room for twelve volunteers. My normal reaction whenever a teacher needs a volunteer is to slowly melt into my chair and try to become invisible. But on this occasion and almost without even knowing I was doing it, I immediately stood up and started walking down to the front of the class. Eleven other volunteers eventually followed suit. As I was standing there, I was saying to myself, "Oh no, no, no, what am I doing?" Then, our teacher pulled out twelve one-hundred dollar bills and began passing out one to each of us. I was trying so hard not to say out loud, "Oh yes, yes, yes, look what I've done!"

As she handed out the money, she said, "Your mission, 'should you decide to accept it,' is to pray very hard about your hundred dollars, and ask God to show you exactly what you need to do with it or who you need to give it to." She told us that in three weeks, each of us would be asked to share with the class how we used the money.

I immediately began to think, "Oh, this will be so easy." I could think of several women right off the top of my head in our recovery class at church who could use the money. I could have easily given it to any one of them, but I wanted to follow the teacher's instructions. I wanted to pray about it and ask God to show me how He wanted me to use the money. I was hoping this experiment would help me feel connected to God again and end my dry spell. I wanted Him to speak to my heart. I wanted to know He was still listening to me when I prayed.

I had been praying for almost two weeks about the money, but still did not feel like I had any clear direction on what to do with the hundred-dollar bill. Then, one day while I was at work, I received a telephone call telling me a young father who had been attending our recovery class at church overdosed on drugs and died. I could not believe it. I had just recently seen him, together with his wife and young children.

His wife, Angie, was devastated. She asked if Ed and I would come to her home before the children returned from school so we would be there when she broke the terrible news to them. I had this overwhelming feeling that Angie was "the one" who was meant to have the hundred dollars. I prayed silently, "Is it her, Lord?" Though I heard no verbal confirmation, I knew in my heart she was the one.

I explained to my boss what happened and asked to leave early that day. When I was gathering up my purse and things to leave the office, I realized I did not have the hundred-dollar bill with me. I had put the bill in my Bible and my Bible was at home. Though I was so disappointed about that, I knew I would see Angie again the next day and I would simply give it to her then.

As I was leaving the office, I heard my boss call my name. I turned around, and he pulled a hundred-dollar bill out of his wallet and said, "I've been thinking about that young mother who just lost her husband. Please take this money and give it to her. Maybe it will help." I was speechless. I thought to myself, "God, you are so amazing." Even though I left my hundred-dollar bill in my Bible, God provided a hundred dollars through someone else. When I gave the money to Angie that evening, she was so very grateful.

The next day, as I prepared to leave work and go back to Angie's home, I realized (and could not believe) I had again forgotten to get the hundred-dollar bill out of my Bible. However, just at that time, a friend and co-worker of mine, Diane, came into my office. She said, "I have had a hundred dollar bill stuck back in my wallet since Christmas. I have been just holding on to it, but after hearing about Angie, I want you to give it to her." I almost fell out of my chair! Neither Diane nor my boss knew about the hundred dollars I had in my Bible for Angie, and neither of them knew about the other one giving me money for Angie. The next day, I finally remembered the money in my Bible, but I have wondered many times who else God would have provided had I forgotten it again.

For three days in a row, I was able to give Angie a hundred dollar bill. She was overwhelmed with gratitude. She had so many unexpected expenses due to her husband's untimely death and the money came at just the right time. My dry spell had ended. There was no doubt in my mind or my heart that God heard my prayers and that He provided the three hundred dollars for Angie.

I tell you this story because it reminds me that when Ed was in the height of his addiction and my life was falling apart, I prayed a lot, and I prayed long. I practiced the "P.U.S.H." method . . . "Pray Until Something Happens."

Yet, when life became better, my prayers became shorter, less intense. I realized one day that even when I am not in desperate need, I should still be praying strong and long prayers of thanksgiving.

I think God has sometimes allowed me to feel distant from Him, not because *He* needs to know how strong my spiritual walk is (because He knows), but so that *I* will know how strong my spiritual walk is with Him.

Do you ever feel distant from God? There is a saying, "If you don't feel close to God, guess who moved?" Have you moved? If your life is good today, I encourage you to spend time with God on your knees and thank Him for all your blessings. However, if you, like so very many today, are struggling with addiction or living with addiction in your home or, for whatever reason, you are feeling distant from God, don't lose hope and don't stop praying; in fact . . . P.U.S.H.

"Be joyful always, pray continually, give thanks in all circumstances; for this is God's will for you in Christ Jesus" (I Thessalonians 5: 16-18).

CHAPTER 17

You Are Not Alone

*E*d and I had been attending Landmark Church for only a short while when our minister asked Ed to give his testimony. Somehow he found out about Ed's drug addiction and subsequent recovery, and he wanted Ed to share that with the church. Giving his testimony was the last thing Ed wanted to do . . . not only because Ed is not a public speaker, but also because we had finally found a church we both truly loved, and we really did not want to do anything to mess that up. Keep in mind, Ed and I grew up in a very conservative church. It was a church where you would never want anyone to find out about your sins, much

139

less actually stand up in front of the whole congregation and voluntarily tell everyone. That seemed inconceivable to us. Ed did, however, finally agree, and the day came when he would give his testimony. As we drove to church that Sunday morning, Ed asked me (half-jokingly),

"Do you think they will kick us out once they hear about my past?"

I replied (half-jokingly), "I don't think they will kick us out, but I doubt anyone is going to invite us over for lunch today."

When Ed finished his testimony, person after person came up and spoke to him. Some were crying. All were thankful. Some were in recovery themselves, and some wanted to be in recovery. Some had friends, employees, co-workers, spouses, or children who needed to be in recovery. Ed's testimony gave so many people so much hope that day.

Satan wanted us to believe we would be ridiculed and ostracized if Ed gave his testimony. Satan wanted us to believe nothing good could come from sharing our struggles with others. Satan wanted us to believe no one else in our church could relate to our past problems; but, the truth is . . . we were not alone. And no matter what you are struggling with today, you are not alone either.

As we drove home from church that Sunday, my mind went back to another Sunday many, many years ago. I was just a young girl. My father was finally able to get sober and we started attending the conservative church I mentioned earlier. There was a young girl at church with whom I had become friends. She and her mother started attending the church about the same time my family did. Her father did not attend. He, like my father, was also an alcoholic, though I did not realize it at the time.

One Sunday, some of us young kids were sitting in church, close to the back and far from our parents. The congregation had just finished the routine two songs, prayer, another song, and the minister had only been preaching a few minutes when the church door behind us opened, and my friend's father walked in.

When I looked at her father, it reminded me of how my father once looked. He was very thin and red-faced. He walked slowly, as though trying not to stagger, and he sat down just a couple of pews in front of us. He folded his trembling hands in his lap in an attempt to keep them from shaking. As he walked past us, we caught a slight whiff of alcohol. His hair was neatly parted and combed to the side. It looked wet, as though he had just put water on it in an effort to make it lay down. I remember he had on a white button-up shirt and dark pants, but no coat or tie. That was unusual to me at the time because back then, the men wore coats and ties to church and the ladies wore dresses and often hats. Still, he looked as though he had done his very best to look his very best. He seemed old to me. I know now it is just because I was so young. In reality, he was probably only in his late thirties or early forties.

When I saw him, I immediately felt panic. My mind raced to my own father, and I felt overwhelmed with sad memories. I also sensed fear from my friend. Not that she was afraid *of* him, but that she was afraid *for* him.

I looked up at the pulpit, hoping the preacher did not see him come in, but of course he did. Some of the men in the church sensed something was wrong by the glances from the preacher towards them, and they turned to see what was going on. Then, the unbelievable happened.

Two of the men rose from their seats and walked to the back of the church. One of them leaned down and whispered something to my friend's father, and he got up and followed the men out of the building. After about ten minutes, the two "church men" came back in and returned to their seats, but my friend's father never returned. In fact, I never saw him or my friend and her mother ever again after that day.

So many times over the years, I have wondered about that man. I have often thought about all the courage it must have taken him to walk through the church doors that day. Was that day the turning point in his life? Was that the day he hit rock bottom? Was that the day he was sick and tired of being sick and tired? Was that the day that his desperation for help finally outweighed his desperation to drink? How long did he sit in the parking lot of the church building before he was brave enough to walk in? Yet, on that day, he was escorted out of the one place he sought to find hope. I wonder if he ever dared enter a church building again. I pray he did, but fear he did not. It makes me cry just to think about him, not only because he was my friend's father, but because he could have easily been my father, too.

I am thankful that Ed and I attend a church today that is a long, long way from the church I attended as a child. I am thankful we attend a church that is full of grace and hope, where no one is perfect, where people freely confess their sins, are not afraid to ask for prayers, and where they know they are not alone.

As a child, I did not understand addiction and alcoholism. All I knew was my father drank too much. We swept everything under the rug and didn't talk about it among ourselves, and we definitely did not share it with others. Being the child of an alcoholic always made me feel different, "less than," and often alone.

As I write this chapter, I can still feel my friend's fear when her father walked into the church building that day, and I can feel her overwhelming sadness when he was led out. I would give anything if I could turn back the clock to that Sunday many years ago and tell my young friend, "My dad is like your dad. I know your fear, I feel your sadness, and you are not alone."

"Two are better than one, because they have a good return for their work:

If one falls down, his friend can help him up. But pity the man who falls and has no one to help him up"
(Ecclesiastes 4:9-10).

CHAPTER 18

The Mirror

*T*his is a chapter Ed should be writing, not me. I remember the first time he gave his testimony in our church. There was not a dry eye in the congregation when he finished speaking. He talked about how far down drugs had taken him and about his last days of active addiction. There are some things that you have to "live" to be able to fully describe them to someone else. I cannot do his story justice, but I will do my best.

Ed's last week of active addiction came on the tail of a strong relapse that engulfed him and caused him to simply leave and not make it back home. He was staying at a cheap motel in a very rough part of town. By this time, his addiction was so full-blown that he could not "not use." He once described his addiction to cocaine as "a bear on my back that I cannot get off." The only good thing at this point was that Ed was no longer in denial. He knew he had a very serious drug problem.

At this phase in his addiction, life for him was almost unbearable. He had already been through treatment, both in-house and outpatient, attended many, many recovery classes, and had been to numerous NA and AA meetings, yet he continued to relapse. He could have taught the class on recovery, yet his own efforts at stopping had failed time and time again. He knew exactly what to do, but actually doing it was another thing. I have heard Ed tell people, "You can be all 'around' recovery and never really be 'in' recovery." He was all around recovery.

That night in the seedy motel room, Ed finally hit what most addicts know as "rock bottom." He had lost his wife and children, his home, his business, his friends, his finances and most of all, his relationship with God.

In this last relapse, he had been using drugs for about five days straight and not eating or sleeping. In the wee hours of the morning, just before dawn, he had become so violently ill that he was not sure he would live to see daylight. His whole body was shutting down. As he lay in bed, he began to continuously shake from strong chills and then the nausea started again. He tried so hard to lie still, hoping the nausea would leave. The thought of the excruciating pain from dry heaves made him even sicker.

The small room was dimly lit. His nausea finally forced him to get out of bed and go into the bathroom. When he came out of the bathroom, he braced himself on the dresser as he tried to make it back to the disheveled bed. It was then that he caught a glimpse of himself in the mirror on the dresser. It had been a long time since Ed had really looked at himself. He stared in disbelief.

As Ed got to this part of his story when giving his testimony, he paused as he tried to compose himself. His voice began to quiver. You could have heard a pin drop in the church. He gathered his composure and said, "That night in the motel when I saw myself in the mirror, I could not believe the person I had become. I no longer recognized myself. I was once a good man, a good father, and a good husband. Now I was a drug addict on the verge of death. Drug addiction had literally taken over my life." He paused again, trying hard to keep it together, and then continued,

"When I saw myself in that mirror, I dropped to my knees on that motel floor and cried out to God to help me. I begged God to take the obsession for drugs away. I did not want to die on drugs in that motel room." He promised God that if He would help him get off the drugs, he would turn his life over to God. When he finally got up off his knees and made it back to bed, he said, "It felt like I was sleeping in the arms of Jesus that night."

From that day forward, Ed never used drugs again. It was not easy, but he became serious about his recovery. He finally got "in recovery" and not just "around recovery." He got a sponsor, he started working the Twelve Steps, and on a daily basis he began turning his life and will over to the care of God.

I have heard of people who believe that God instantly and miraculously delivered them from their addiction, and I believe them. However, most of the addicts who I personally know have been delivered from addiction by using the tools God provides through the Twelve Steps of groups such as AA and NA.

Jesus preformed many miracles in the Bible. Some people were instantly healed when they touched Him; some were instantly healed when He touched them; some were healed when He simply spoke the words; yet, there were those who were healed only after they personally did certain things required of them. One example of this is when God required the leper to dip in the Jordan River seven times before he was cleansed of his leprosy. Could God have healed the leper without any effort on the leper's part? Absolutely. But God, in His great wisdom, sometimes heals people in different ways.

Ed is one of those who God has healed through AA and NA. However, I believe that Ed is no less of a miracle than someone whom God healed instantly. I believe with all my heart that God has delivered Ed from drugs . . . today. And if Ed continues to do what he is supposed to do, God will deliver Ed from drugs tomorrow. I believe that each day Ed gets up and turns his life and his will over to the care of God and does the things that he needs to do to stay clean and sober, God gives Ed a daily reprieve from his addiction.

Ed gives God all the glory for his sobriety, but he also will tell you today that he is still a recovering addict. It reminds me of the story in the Bible about the impure spirit who comes out of a person. Matthew 12:43-45 says, "It goes through arid places seeking rest and does not find it. Then it says, 'I will return to the house I left.' When it arrives, it finds the house swept clean and put in order. Then it goes and takes seven other spirits more wicked than itself, and they go in and live there. And the final condition of that person is worse than the first." In other words, we can clean up our lives, our language, our hearts, but if we don't replace the bad with something good, the bad can return with a vengeance. Being a recovering addict is like that. You need a "maintenance program."

Ed and I had a friend who is now deceased. His name is Tom Brady. Tom was a renowned author, speaker and a recovering alcoholic who had been clean for decades. He often traveled around the country speaking to groups about addiction and sharing the hope of recovery. He is the author of a book titled *Thirsting for Wholeness*. I love that title.

It's a great book about addiction and recovery, but it is even a greater book about how most people, addicts or not, are "thirsting for wholeness," trying to fill a void in their lives that only Christ can fill. I will always remember the following statement Tom once made: "There will come a time in every addict's life when, no matter how long he has been clean or sober, the only thing that will keep him clean or sober, will be his spiritual walk with God."

I believe the above is so true of Ed. For the past nineteen years, Ed has kept his promise to God. His spiritual walk has been strong. Ed starts every day with prayer and meditation. He ends every night on his knees in thanksgiving. I have heard Ed tell many people that no matter what the day may bring, if he is walking in God's will, everything will be "just right." It may not always be just the way Ed always wants it to be, but it is "just right."

God has used Ed for things that only someone who has been through the hell of drug addiction could be used for. There is no doubt that God had a plan for him.

Ed ended his testimony in church that day by saying, "It is my prayer that one day God will open up the gates of heaven and let me in. But this I know for sure . . . in the wee hours of the morning in a dirty motel room when I was dying on drugs, God opened up the gates of hell and let me out."

"The Lord is near to all who call upon Him, to all who call upon Him in truth. He fulfills the desires of those who fear Him; He hears their cry and saves them" (Psalm 145: 18-19).

CHAPTER 19

Waiting

To put it bluntly . . . I hate to wait. I don't like to think of myself as an impatient person, it is just that for me, with waiting often comes much anxiety. The truth is, I have spent most of my life waiting. As a child, I waited for Christmas, waited for my first tooth to fall out, waited for school to start, waited on the school bus, waited for school to end, and waited to turn sixteen so I could drive. When I became a mother, I spent most of my time waiting in doctor offices, waiting for school to start, waiting for the school bus, waiting for school to end, waiting for teenage boys to come home, and waiting for the dryer to go off. Then, of course, there is the waiting in line at the grocery store, often maneuvering from line to line to make sure I was in the shortest line. Ever done that?

The hardest waiting I ever did was waiting for my husband to come home and not knowing if he was even coming home at all. Waiting has caused my heart to run, my mind to race, my head to hurt and my blood pressure to rise. The good news is—waiting also gave me time to slow down, time to reflect, time to focus, and time to pray. However, after I prayed, I was back to waiting. Waiting for an answer, waiting for a sign . . . waiting for "my" will to be done. What a cycle! Ever been there?

I have come to believe one of the primary reasons we, as believers, step out of God's will for us, fall out of fellowship with the Lord, and rush into making wrong decisions, is because we do not wait on God's timing for us. Waiting on the Lord does not mean doing nothing. I believe it means we just need to slow down, pause, pray and wait until we receive further instructions.

We live in a fast world—an "instant" world where we are used to having everything at the push of a button. We often fear if we do not take advantage of an opportunity right away, we might miss out. So we too often jump into something without taking time to truly wait for God's answer and for direction from God.

There are many, many verses in the Bible about patience and waiting. One of my favorite is Psalm 27:14, *"Wait for the Lord; be strong and take heart, and wait for the Lord."* Did you notice in that one single verse, God tells us not once, but twice, to wait for the Lord? Do you think He knows how impatient we are?

Through my ordeal with Ed and his addiction, I found that waiting strengthened my faith. I have to admit I often waited because I simply ran out of other options and had nothing else to try. But there was one time when I intentionally waited, and the reward from waiting proved to be worth it. I am speaking of the time when I waited to divorce Ed. Oh, believe me, I *wanted* to divorce him. And had he not changed, divorce would have been my only option; but I waited.

At the time, I could not understand why I was waiting. I certainly had reasons to divorce Ed. For all intents and purposes my marriage was over. Because of his addiction, I endured a broken heart, broken family, broken bank accounts and broken vows. My family and friends would have surely understood my decision to divorce him. In fact, some of them even encouraged it. Because I worked for a divorce attorney, attorney's fees were not a problem. Custody of our children was not an issue, and we had no money, property, or assets left to "divvy up." Still, I waited.

Many, many times I had the urge to divorce him. I wanted to just "kick him to the curb" and start all over. Yet, every time I sat down to type up the divorce papers, something deep down inside me kept saying, "Wait." So I waited. I found that as I waited, I began to grow stronger. Isaiah 40:31 tells us, "Those who wait upon the Lord will gain new strength." God was strengthening me.

Remember me telling you of the night in the trailer when I had fallen on my knees, broken and prayed with all my heart for God to help me? And remember me telling you about the night that Ed had fallen on his knees in that dirty motel room, broken and prayed with all his heart for God to help him? Well, it was the same night. Coincidence? Not a chance.

I often envision the Lord whispering to me that night, "Wait. Surrender to me, and I will help you through this." And I envision the Lord whispering to Ed that night, "Why wait? Surrender to me, and I will help you through this."

I am so thankful today that I waited. Waiting gives you time to change your heart, change your mind, change your direction, and seek out God's will. But if we are to know His will for us, we must know Him; and if we are to know Him, we must know His word. We need to sift all of our cares, worries, and concerns about our life through His word.

Are you in the process of making a hasty decision today about something you should wait and pray about? Are you waiting on something today, yet filled with anxiety? Are you waiting for the check in the mail? Your ship to come in? Your spouse to come home? If you are waiting and relying on your own efforts and your own strength, it will leave you empty and unfulfilled.

In Psalm 130:5 we read, "I wait for the Lord, my soul waits, and in his word, I put my hope." It is my prayer for you and for me that we always put our hope in His word and our trust in a caring God whose love for us is always present, always secure, and never ending.

If you are in the midst of a trial right now and are uncertain what to do, wait on Him, lean on Him, trust in Him. He can change your heart, change your path . . . change your life.

"Wait for the Lord; be strong and take heart, and wait for the Lord" (Psalm 27:14).

CHAPTER 20

Hope

$\mathcal{M}$any years ago, I was asked by someone in our church to speak at one of our ladies' retreats. Before then, I had never stood up in front of a large group of people and shared my story. I was so nervous. We met in a large banquet room. We were served a wonderful meal, and then it came time for me to speak. I remember I could hardly hear myself think for my heart pounding in my chest. I did the best I could at the time, but back then the pain of everything was still pretty fresh. I am afraid I might have vented more than I testified.

What I really want to tell you is not about my testimony that night, but what happened afterwards. All of us women gathered in another room where the chairs were set up in a large circle. When we entered the room, each woman was handed an unlit candle. As soon as we were all seated, someone turned the power off and it was pitch black. After a few minutes, the leader of the group lit her small candle. Even with her candle lit, you could just barely see her face. Then our session began.

She talked about what a dark, dark world we would live in if we did not have hope. She spoke of the importance of sharing our faith, hope and strength with others. She then stood up and walked across the room to another woman and said to her, "I will never forget the night you came to my house and prayed with me after hearing of my diagnosis. You had walked in my shoes before, you had felt my fear, you were cancer free then and you gave me hope." When she finished speaking, she lit the woman's candle and went and sat down. The room became a tad bit brighter.

The woman whose candle she lit then stood up and walked to a woman who was much older than she and said, "Thank you for mentoring to me when I was just a young wife and young mother. You shared your experience with me. You taught me about love and about patience. You made me a better wife to my husband and a better mama to my little girl."

She then lit the woman's candle with her candle and the room became a little brighter. The older woman then took her candle and walked over to another woman and said, "All the cards and telephone calls from you when my husband was terminally ill gave me strength to get through each day. I love and thank you for that." She lit that woman's candle and the room became a little brighter. You see where this is going. Each woman, time and time again, took her candle that was lit by someone she encouraged and in turn she lit the candle of someone who had encouraged her. When it was all said and done, the room was so bright from the candles that it looked as though the power had been turned back on. And, in fact, it had been ". . . the power of faith, the power of hope, the power of love."

I cannot stress enough the importance of hope when you are dealing with addiction. I know what hopelessness feels like and I know what hopelessness looks like. I have seen it in the eyes of mothers, fathers, husbands, wives, siblings, and friends. I do not claim to be an expert on addiction, but one thing I have come to learn and feel certain of is that there is always hope. I am not saying that every addict or alcoholic turns into a success story, because sadly, that is not the case. But we should never lose hope for them, and we should never lose hope for ourselves.

There are people I know and love who still struggle with addiction. It is my most fervent prayer that those still active in addiction find help . . . and never lose hope. But it is also my prayer that those of us who love and lose friends and family members to addiction, sometimes even to the point of death, know that there is still hope.

Today, my hope is in God. Though life does not always go the way we want, He is faithful to help us through our most difficult situations and our most heartbreaking times. Remember that no matter what we go through on this earth, it is only temporary. I have lived long enough to know that life is not always fair and that there will be questions that we will never have the answers to . . . this side of heaven. It took me a long time to accept that, but eventually I did. I know today that God never leaves me or forsakes me and that no matter what troubles or heartaches I face, they are only temporary. He tells us, "For our light and momentary troubles are achieving for us an eternal glory that far outweighs them all." (2 Corinthians 4:17). God's promise, not mine.

Remember that we are all on the journey "home." I pray that you never give up, that you never lose hope, and may we all light someone's candle along the way.

"Therefore we do not lose heart. Though outwardly we are wasting away, yet inwardly we are being renewed day by day. For our light and momentary troubles are achieving for us an eternal glory that far outweighs them all. So we fix our eyes not on what is seen, but on what is unseen. For what is seen is temporary, but what is unseen is eternal" (2 Corinthians 4:16-18).

CHAPTER 21

Today

I personally do not know anyone who has more passion or more compassion than Ed when it comes to recovery. When Ed got clean and sober, he knew he wanted to help other addicts and alcoholics. Recovery was like a miracle gift that had been given to him, and he just had to share it with others.

Ed did some checking and found out there were only a couple of halfway houses for men in our town at that time. Every Monday evening, Ed would pick up pizzas and take them to the men at one of the halfway houses. After he won the men over with the food, Ed would talk to them about sobriety and recovery. He would have a devotional with them and pray for them.

This sort of kindness and goodness was very strange to most of the men. They were not used to this kind of caring or compassion. Week after week, and year after year, Ed faithfully showed up with pizzas and a Bible; and week after week, the men showed up not only to eat, but also to be spiritually fed.

Ed would come home from the halfway house and tell me how bad the living conditions were there. He talked about the few old pieces of damaged furniture these men had, the peeling paint in the house, the leaky roof, and the roaches. One might think these men brought this situation on themselves, and surely they did. But to Ed, some of these men deserved "one more second chance," and he began dreaming of having a better place in which to offer that second chance. I said "some" because Ed is a firm believer that you have to want recovery. No one can give it to you or force it on you. You have to work for it. Some of these men truly wanted it, and were willing to work for it.

When Ed first brought up the idea to me of opening up a home for recovering addicts and alcoholics, I was scared to death. We were not even back on our feet financially, and

I had no idea how we would ever be able to do this. Plus, part of me just wanted to distance myself from anything and everything that had to do with addiction. Ed, on the other hand, was on a mission, and he was determined that if it was God's will, he was going to open up a home for men. He did not want it to be called a "halfway house." He wanted it to be called a "recovery home." We prayed and prayed about it. I knew Ed had so much to offer to other men struggling with addictions, so I agreed.

In 2003, the property was purchased; and in February 2004, "The Shed" was opened as a private spiritual and residential recovery home for men. The name "SHED" represents the following goals of the home: "Shelter, Healing, Education, and Development." The Shed provides housing, assistance in job placement, transportation, counseling, structure, and spiritual guidance. Today we have grown to four houses, each next door to the other.

Prior to opening The Shed, Ed and I started a Twelve Step program at our church for addicts and their family members to attend. It started very slowly. Sometimes we had one or two in the class, and sometimes only Ed and I showed up. Before we would leave, we would always pray for "the empty chair." As word got out, the class began to grow more and more; and in 2000, Ed and his dear friends, Tim and David, began the recovery class at our church known as "RSVP" (Recovery, Sponsorship, Victorious Living, and Prayer.) It is not uncommon to have fifty or more people in that class on Wednesday evenings. And every Wednesday evening before class starts, you will find Ed and some of the men from The Shed in our church kitchen, cooking a meal for all those who show up for "RSVP." Ed truly has the gift of a servant's heart and he also knows this meal could be the best meal some of them will have all week.

A lot of good men and women, young and old, have attended the RSVP class over the years. And a lot of men, young and old, have resided at The Shed over the years. Although not everyone has been a success story, many have. Ed once told me, "We are not in charge of the results, God is. We are simply here to serve and plant the seeds of recovery."

I look back and think of all the times I asked God to change our circumstances and to take away all the hurt caused by Ed's addiction. Yet today I know that I am stronger because of it. I am also so thankful that God, in His great wisdom, did not answer all of my prayers because had some things been done *my* way, I would have sold myself so short.

It is like the country song by Garth Brooks . . . "I could have missed the pain, but I would have had to miss the dance."

On May 15, 2013, Ed celebrated nineteen years of sobriety. I can remember all the times when I thought Ed would never recover. Oh, me of little faith. As I look back, I see so much good that came from so much bad. I see how God took what Satan intended for evil and used it for His glory.

Today, Ed and I do our best to turn our lives and our wills over to the care of God. I do not want to insinuate that Ed and I have "arrived," because we are flawed. We always have been and always will be. But I thank God for His unconditional love, His amazing grace and His great mercy.

Ed's addiction took us down many roads and many turns. Although the road of addiction is not a road I would have dreamed our lives would have ever taken, I learned a lot about myself while on this journey.

I learned that I am not defined by the things I own, the stuff I possess, or the place I live. I learned that life can change in a heartbeat. I learned who my true friends are. I learned to be more grateful. More than anything, I learned that our heavenly Father is a faithful, kind, loving and good God . . . all the time.

Today, I feel blessed. As I reflect back over the years, good and bad, I can honestly say, "I wouldn't take 'nothin' for my journey now." Of course, if you ask Ed how he is doing today, he will tell you, "Just right."

"I know the plans I have for you," declares the Lord, "plans to prosper you and not to harm you, plans to give you hope and a future" (Jeremiah 29:11-12).

ABOUT THE AUTHOR

arbara and Ed reside in Alabama and have attended Landmark Church in Montgomery for the past sixteen years. They will celebrate forty-three years of marriage in December 2013. They have three sons, three daughters-in-law (like daughters to them) and four grandchildren.

Please visit Barbara's web page at www.justrightbook.com.

CPSIA information can be obtained at www.ICGtesting.com
Printed in the USA
LVOW11s0150251013

358477LV00001B/1/P